Praise for
SOBER MERCIES

"SOBER MERCIES is a delightful and brave read. Heather Kopp's narrative, full of gut-wrenching detail and heartfelt confession, is beautifully crafted, a story filled with the kind of self-reflection and wisdom reminiscent of Anne Lamott and Mary Karr. And like the works of Lamott and Karr, the true gift of Kopp's tale is that every reader—addict or not—will find its honesty and hope filling."
—Matthew Paul Turner, author of *Churched* and *Hear No Evil*

"SOBER MERCIES is simply one of the best, most honest, brilliantly written memoirs I've read. Heather Kopp gives such encouragement for when we wonder why faith alone hasn't rescued us from destructive habits. Her story stands as a beacon of hope for all of us in a broken world." —Jud Wilhite, author of *Pursued*, senior pastor of Central Christian Church

"I loved SOBER MERCIES. Kopp is funny, heartbreaking, compelling, and wise. More than that, this is an important book. Kopp talks frankly about being a Christian *and* an alcoholic. This book is a must for any recovery group or anyone facing addiction."
—Susan E. Isaacs, actor, author of *Angry Conversations with God*

"I couldn't put this book down, devouring it in a weekend. Even people who have never struggled with addiction will find themselves in Heather Kopp's memoir of finding God's strength only when she recognized her own powerlessness. As she says, it's about 'how to lean—helplessly, foolishly, hopefully—on a God you can't fully explain. And how to do it, over and over, every day.'"
—Jana Riess, author of *Flunking Sainthood: A Year of Breaking the Sabbath, Forgetting to Pray,* and *Still Loving My Neighbor*

"Taught prose, a compelling story, and a beautifully fresh voice kept me turning the pages of SOBER MERCIES. This is not a pretty story. It's not another well-decorated memoir where the author glosses over failure and stress. Heather Kopp's story is raw. Her bravery will give others the permission to grow, change, and heal."

—Mary DeMuth, author of *Thin Places: A Memoir*

"In SOBER MERCIES, Heather Kopp's soft wisdom is delivered so skillfully that it continued to settle in days and weeks after I read the last page. Heather's vision of Christianity is vast, inclusive, and interesting. Her journey is hilarious, and inspiring and her honesty is both surprising and comforting. I plan to keep extra copies of SOBER MERCIES on my bookshelf, ready to give to any friend struggling with faith, recovery, forgiveness, or life. So, I'll give it to everyone, I guess. I love this book. SOBER MERCIES is a gift and Heather Kopp is my favorite kind of person: a student-turned-teacher of life."

—Glennon Doyle Melton, founder of Momastery.com, author of *Carry On, Warrior*

"This is not a book for alcoholics, or a book for friends and family of addicts, or a book for counselors, or a book for women; it's a book for everyone. Heather's story—honestly and beautifully told—invites us all to the table, baggage in tow, to confront our shared brokenness, our shared hopes, and our shared need for community, forgiveness, and grace. This book will challenge and change you. It will reintroduce you, with new words and images and stories, to the grace and goodness of God."

—Rachel Held Evans, blogger, author of *Evolving in Monkey Town* and *A Year of Biblical Womanhood*

SOBER MERCIES

*How Love Caught Up with
a Christian Drunk*

HEATHER KOPP

JERICHO
BOOKS ™

New York   Boston   Nashville

All Biblical quotations are taken from Today's New International Version, copyright © 2001, 2005 by International Bible Society.

Jericho Books
Hachette Book Group
237 Park Avenue
New York, NY 10017

JerichoBooks.com

Printed in the United States of America

RRD-C

First Edition: May 2013
10 9 8 7 6 5 4 3 2 1

Jericho Books is an imprint of FaithWords.
The Jericho Books name and logo are trademarks of Hachette Book Group, Inc.

The Hachette Speakers Bureau provides a wide range of authors for speaking events. To find out more, go to www.HachetteSpeakersBureau.com or call (866) 376-6591.

The publisher is not responsible for websites (or their content) that are not owned by the publisher.

Library of Congress Cataloging-in-Publication Data
Kopp, Heather Harpham, 1964-
  Sober mercies : how love caught up with a christian drunk / Heather Harpham Kopp.
      p. cm. ISBN 978-1-4555-2774-8 (hardcover)—ISBN 978-1-4555-2773-1 (ebook) 1. Kopp, Heather Harpham, 1964-
2. Christian biography. 3. Alcoholics—Religious life. I. Title.
  BR1725.K665A3 2013
  248.8'6292092—dc23
  [B]   2012033554

For those who still suffer.

AUTHOR'S NOTE

In some instances I changed minor details and identifying characteristics to protect the privacy of people I'd rather not name. However, my family of origin and immediate family are called by their real names, and they graciously supported my decision to tell this story.

Most recovery programs have a tradition of anonymity, since no single person can or should represent or speak for such a group. For that reason, I don't name the specific community that helps me stay sober, and I hope you'll refrain from publically associating my name or this story with any particular organization.

CONTENTS

CONTENTS

SOBER MERCIES

PART ONE

WAKING UP IN THE GUEST ROOM

I know where I am before I open my eyes. I can tell by the pillow, which is too soft and mushy to be my normal pillow. It means I slept in the guest room again last night. It's a realization so awful that I quickly will myself to stay asleep, to hurry back to oblivion. But it's too late. I'm fully conscious now. I roll over, my face in the pillow, and wish I had the courage to smother myself.

This is the second time it's happened this month. As usual, I don't know how I got here, but I can guess why. I search my brain for a scrap of memory about the previous evening, but there is none. I can't recall a single thing after around seven p.m. My husband, Dave, and I had gone downtown for dinner. I ordered a shrimp salad and Chardonnay. I probably drank a couple mini wines in the ladies' room.

I don't remember us leaving the restaurant, much less getting into a huge fight. But there's no other explanation. I glance at the clock. He's at work already. I get up and stumble into the bathroom, where I pause to stare with hate at my face in the mirror. My skin is so puffy that my eye sockets bulge like lemons with small slits.

Obviously, I was crying a lot last night. But about what? What did Dave do?

Or rather, what horrible thing did I decide or imagine Dave did—after I got drunk and irrational?

Twice, I have seen scratches on him in the morning. His face. His neck. Dear God, let it not be that bad this time.

Later, I sit down to write an e-mail to Dave to apologize. I can't bear to wait until he gets home from work to face him, my shame flaming. As usual, I try to sound sincere in my note, to take the full blame, but I have to be intentionally vague. I can't let on that I have absolutely no idea what we fought about last night, or how bad it was.

I will have to look for clues in his response.

one

CRISIS IN KMART

I never saw the end of my drinking days coming.

But then again, maybe most alcoholics don't. By the time the end comes, we're so attached to our addiction that if we knew what person, event, or twist of fate was going to eventually result in our deliverance, like a drowning person who fights her rescuer, we'd do everything in our power to make sure it never happened.

So instead, God comes to us disguised as our life, wooing us through our misery toward surrender.

At least, that was how it was for me.

When I trace my story back to find the beginning of the end of my drinking, I arrive at a wedding. It was September 2006, and Dave's best friend, Larry, was getting married to an actress and writer from Los Angeles.

I met Susan for the first time at her rehearsal dinner, the night before her wedding. She struck me as bright, funny, and down to earth. I liked her zany, irreverent style. She and Larry exchanged vows the following day, and as they shimmied back down the aisle to James Brown's "I Feel Good," I had high hopes for a friendship with her.

Soon after, Susan and Larry came to visit us for a weekend. They arrived on a brisk but sunny fall afternoon. We all sat in the living room and chatted about how amazing it was that Larry at fifty, and Susan, in her forties, had finally found one another (it was a first marriage for both)—and through an online dating site, no less.

After a while, the four of us bundled up in coats and hats and took a walk through the tiny Central Oregon town where Dave and I were living at the time. As we strolled past gift shops and tourist boutiques, Susan regaled us with funny stories about acting auditions gone wrong. I particularly loved the one where she tried out for a diaper commercial by crawling around on the floor like a baby.

We got back to the house around five o'clock. Since our dinner reservations at a nearby restaurant weren't until seven p.m., I did what any good hostess would do: I opened up a nice bottle of white wine and put out a cheese plate for my guests to snack on. That was when it happened.

Susan said, "Do you have any tea?"

I stared at her blankly, willing her to take it back.

"Actually," she added, "if you have hot water, I brought my own loose leaf."

Her request instantly brought to mind another couple Dave and I had visited in their home in Ashland, Oregon. Upon our arrival, this husband and wife cheerily explained that after developing bad martini habits, they had both quit drinking. "We have tea for happy hour now!" they exclaimed.

They said this as if it were good news. As if they had no idea (which they didn't) that I could never subsist for several days on the limited amount of alcohol that was hidden in my suitcase. The extra four-packs of mini wine I'd brought were meant to *supplement* the generous amount of alcohol I had expected to be served by our hosts.

I don't know how I made it through. I think we left a day early. And now, here was Susan, saying it again: *Tea!*

Later at the restaurant, my worst fears about Susan were confirmed when she ordered tea with her dinner, and casually confided, "I don't drink."

My heart sank. And she had *seemed* so hip, so funny, and likable...

Throughout dinner, and for the rest of Susan's stay, I felt sad about the friendship with her that would never be. But I felt even sorrier for Susan. What would it be like to drink tea with dinner? To wake up every day knowing you were going to feel the same way at seven p.m. as you did at seven a.m.?

It was a life of such vast meaninglessness I couldn't wrap my head around it.

৬

By the time I met Susan, I knew I was an alcoholic. It was something I'd been feverishly working to hide for almost twelve years. Of course, Dave knew I had a serious drinking problem. But even he still had no idea that in addition to the three or four glasses of wine he saw me drink each evening, I was covertly consuming several times that amount from a secret stash in my closet.

Lately, however, the constant effort it took just to keep this stash stocked at all times had come to seem like a part-time job. The covert shopping trips, the rounding up of the hidden empties, and the weekly unpacking and repacking of the garbage can on pick-up days had left me demoralized and exhausted.

Worse, I was starting to get sloppy. I felt like bottles were literally spilling out of my life. One morning, I was getting breakfast in the kitchen with Dave when he noticed a lump in the pocket of my robe. "What's that?" he asked, gesturing at it.

I pulled out an empty mini wine bottle, acting as if I was as surprised by its presence as he was. "Oh, wow," I said with a chuckle. "It's just an old bottle from way back when. Guess I need to wash my robe more often..."

He let that go. But lately, things like this had been happening a lot. I'd stumble upon a bottle I'd stashed somewhere stupid or obvious, aghast but grateful I was lucky enough to find it first. How much longer could I hope to keep this up?

Soon after Susan and Larry's "tea," the small publishing company where Dave had worked for many years was sold. The new owners planned to relocate it from Oregon to Colorado Springs. Eager to keep Dave on staff, they invited us to fly there for an exploratory visit.

The day after we flew into town, Dave was scheduled to be in meetings all afternoon with company executives. Later, we were slated to have dinner at a fancy restaurant with the president, the vice president of editorial, and their wives. Not wanting to hang around the hotel, I asked Dave to drop me off at a shopping mall so I could buy a new outfit for the evening.

I'd been wandering stores, casually shopping for several hours before I realized my mistake. How could I be so stupid? We were planning to follow the publisher and his wife straight to the restaurant after Dave picked me up at the mall, but I had failed to transfer some of the mini wines hidden in my suitcase into the center pocket of my large purse.

How was I going to *drink*?

At this stage of my alcoholism, my tolerance was so high I required at least several glasses of wine in the late afternoon just to feel *normal*. Which meant that by the time we got to the restaurant, I'd be ready to crawl out of my skin. Worse, this was exactly the kind of social situation I found excruciating in any state. Plus, these were Christians. Even if they drank, a polite glass or two of wine would hardly suffice.

I told myself not to panic. I would simply have to find some alcohol between now and when Dave picked me up at the appointed time in front of Sears. I had less than forty-five minutes.

I began to walk the mall with great purpose. Surely, I could find one of those specialty gift shops that feature local, high-end products, including wine. I was also prepared to buy a bottle opener if I had to. After wasting about ten minutes looking for such a place, I finally found a mall directory. I quickly scanned it. None of the stores listed resembled what I had in mind. *What kind of mall is this?* I thought.

And then I saw it. A listing for Kmart. *Kmart sells wine!* Back in Oregon, more than once, I had ducked into a Kmart to purchase my little four-packs of mini wine.

I walked toward the pretty red K. I smiled as I entered, remembering when I used to bring my boys here. My first husband and I had been so desperately poor that visiting a discount store had constituted a big outing. Sometimes I'd buy the boys those horrible nachos with fake cheese to keep them happy while I explored the blue-light specials.

Now, for some reason, I couldn't find the wine section. Where were they hiding it? Still unworried, I flagged down an employee, a bald man with a kind face. "Can you point me to your wine aisle?" I asked, all friendliness and optimism.

"What do you mean?"

"*Wine,*" I said, clearly enunciating. "As in wine you drink."

"Gee, ma'am," he said. (And my heart plummeted right there.) "We don't sell wine. In fact, no regular stores in Colorado sell wine. Or liquor. You gotta go to the liquor store for that."

"What?" I said, feeling a little dizzy. "Are you serious?"

He nodded.

What kind of a crazy town was this? Bad enough that it was crawling with the kinds of Christians I once was and now often avoided—but no wine in the grocery store? Were they serious?

Stay calm, I told myself. "Okay," I said with a big breath. "So where is the nearest liquor store?"

"Hmmm," he said, absently twirling the pencil tucked above his ear. "I don't think there's one too near here. But maybe a mile up the road—"

"That's okay," I said, stopping him. "I don't have a car."

He must have noticed the look of distress on my face. "Oh, but wait!" he said, brightening. "You can get that weak kinda beer—the stuff with less alcohol in it, you know—at the grocery store." He smiled like he'd given me a gift.

Did I look that desperate?

I probably did.

"Then again," he added, obviously still thinking, "it's probably a ways to the grocery store, too. But I guess you could walk." He glanced at my feet, in case I was wearing running shoes. I wasn't.

I checked my watch. I didn't have time to walk anywhere. And the Springs is not like New York—taxis don't just pass by. By the time one came...

By now, I was trembling. I thanked the man and rushed to the nearest mall exit to see what I could see outside. In the near distance—a big parking lot and a couple of long blocks away—there appeared to be a gas station with one of those little markets in it. If the grocery stores sold weak beer, maybe the little markets did, too. I set off walking in that direction, readjusting my heavy shopping bags on my shoulder.

I would have to be wearing a sweater. And it would have to be an unusually hot day for late September. By the time I reached the gas station, I was sweating like a pig. But inside the little grocery, it was blessedly cool. I rushed to the back wall where I could see a cold case. And glory! Praise God from whom all blessings flow! I was in luck.

They had no wine. But at least they had beers. I remembered what the guy at Kmart had said. Sure enough, these were *weak* beers. Only 3.2 percent alcohol. I would need a lot of them in order to make a dent big enough to help me get through the evening. Thank God they carried the jumbo 24-ounce size! I cradled five of the cold cans into my arms (beers that big don't come in six-packs) and hurried to the counter.

The cashier, a young guy, looked at me funny. He even asked me for ID and gazed at my Oregon license like I was suspicious. I made up my mind that there was no way we were moving to this stupid town.

The store door dinged as I left the little market and began huffing toward the mall. After half a block, I stopped to cram the big plastic bag of beers into one of my other shopping bags, in case Dave drove by. How would I explain what I was doing out here on the sidewalk with a bag of beer?

Then, I checked my watch. I was almost out of time. I was supposed to meet Dave in ten minutes. I tried to run, but the shopping bags were now agonizingly heavy, the plastic cutting into my palms and shoulders. I could feel perspiration dripping down my back. I cursed the high altitude. I cursed Colorado Springs and their stupid, weak beer.

Then, as Sears came into view, it hit me like a thunderbolt: how was I going to get all these beers into my purse so I could bring them into the restaurant and into the ladies' room so I could drink them? My large three-chambered purse with its center-zip pocket was perfect for hiding four or five mini wines. But it would never in a million years hold all these jumbo beers.

My panic reached a crescendo. I realized that in the few minutes I had left, I would have to find and buy a new, elephant-sized purse. And then be careful to keep it close to me—and away from Dave—all night.

I'll spare you the details of my mad dash to Sears and my frantic speed-shopping. Suffice it to say that when Dave picked me up at the appointed spot, I felt like Wonder Woman. Not only had I managed to buy a humongous purse, I'd accomplished the purse switch in the ladies' room, changed into my new outfit, and guzzled one of the beers in a toilet stall.

I greeted my husband about five minutes late, exhausted, shiny with sweat, chewing hard on two sticks of spearmint gum, and thinking, *How on earth did my life come to this?*

two

PRAISE GOD FOR GRAPES

O nce upon a time, I assumed my Christian faith would make me immune to the kind of gross moral lapse I considered alcoholism to be. The way I saw it, if you were a sincere believer, you would rarely, if ever, drink. And if you did drink, you would be careful not to drink too much. And if you never drank too much, you couldn't become an alcoholic.

It was sound logic, and my experience in my twenties seemed to bear that out. During my first marriage and while my two sons, Noah and Nathan, were little, I rarely drank. Not because I didn't like wine or beer, but because my first husband and I associated drinking with the wild parties of our high school years. Plus, none of our church friends drank.

I've never been able to pinpoint exactly when my thinking on alcohol changed, except to note that it preceded the breakup of my twelve-year marriage. The story of our mostly amicable divorce is too long to tell here, and not all that interesting. Let's just say that he and I were young (we married at seventeen), we came from broken families, and we managed to lose our way.

Headed for divorce, I found myself on the wrong side of a Christian taboo that had guided me for many years. In the past, I had judged plenty of people for taking the "easy way out" by getting divorced. Now, in order to assuage my own guilty conscience, I began to distance myself from the strict ideals and convictions of a Christian community that seemed to be distancing itself from me.

At the time, I would have told you I was tired of being the kind of Christian who was only *against* things. Now, the idea of total abstinence from alcohol struck me as silly and legalistic. I wanted to be a different kind of Christian. The kind who didn't put God in a box. The kind who wasn't sheltered from the real world. And, probably most important, *the kind who drank without apology.*

Meanwhile, I discovered that wine coolers helped to ease the pain of a failed marriage. What possible harm could a Seagram's Peach Fuzzy Navel do?

In retrospect, it was a perfect spiritual storm: a growing cynicism about my faith, guilt about my divorce, and a new affinity for alcohol.

ॐ

When I began to date Dave, he wooed me with flowers, poems— and wine. He introduced me to buttery Chardonnays and rich Merlots, which we sipped while kissing in his kitchen. Drinking was part of the romantic whirlwind of our courtship.

But while we were falling hard for each other, we missed the fact that I was falling hard for alcohol, too.

After we married, Dave and I bought a house large enough for our new blended family. Dave's three kids (Neil, Taylor, and Jana) and my two (Noah and Nathan) were all between the ages of nine and fourteen.

Jana and Nathan—our youngest—were happy, optimistic types who adored each other from the start. Taylor and Noah—the middle two—could spend days locked in a room watching sports or playing video games together. Neil, the oldest, brought a helpful, calming presence, despite his aspirations to grow up to be a mobster.

To my surprise, their interactions with us and with each other were almost entirely without the kind of rancor you might expect in a blended family. But still, a combined family is a challenge. In our case, both sets of kids now had two homes and two sets of parents (my first husband remarried six months after I did). Almost every weekend Dave or I or both of us had to drive over a mountain pass to transport our kids to or from our exes' homes.

For all the good we shared, it was a stressful time of life.

As a holdover from our dating days, Dave and I quickly developed the habit of having a bottle of wine with dinner. It seemed like the natural, civilized thing to do. Drinking was a way to celebrate the good life God had given us. We wouldn't dream of inviting friends over without popping a cork.

For Dave, this lifestyle worked fine, since he's not an alcoholic. But what neither of us knew yet was that I was. The more I drank, the more I wanted to drink. And more was never enough. *Who gets the last glass? Can I open another bottle?*

I praised God for grapes. I decided drinking made any bad thing bearable and any good thing great.

Dave didn't agree. Before long, he began to express disapproval about how much I drank. At first, he did it sweetly. He made references to what was "appropriate" or "smart." If we planned to have company, he'd caution me ahead of time, "Maybe we [meaning *you*] should take it easy with the drinking tonight, hon."

I brushed him off, annoyed and embarrassed. Even so, I couldn't help noticing he was right about the consistent difference in our appetites for alcohol. How come I always wanted to drink more than he did? Maybe I just liked the taste of alcohol more. Or maybe a woman's body processed it differently.

Or maybe Dave was just a stick in the mud. That had to be it!

What I knew of Dave's upbringing seemed to support this theory. The son of Christian missionary parents to Africa, Dave was born in Northern Rhodesia, under British rule at the time. From the age of five, he attended a Plymouth Brethren boarding school, where he learned good manners from a brutally strict headmaster. Christian piety converged with British propriety every morning as little David sang, "God Save the Queen," and then recited a Bible verse from memory.

When I first learned about Dave's childhood, it helped to explain why he could seem so politely reserved. People often commented that he was a bit enigmatic. Extremely gracious and welcoming of others, he was slow to reveal much about himself. When I was unhappy, this trait reinforced my assessment that he was withholding and arrogant.

And yet, what some might call Dave's fatherly demeanor was also part of what had attracted me to him in the first place. Combined with his being fifteen years my senior, he seemed mature and wise—a man in full, not a boy. I admired him. Always, the little girl inside of me desperately craved his approval.

So, when Dave joked about the empty pizza boxes he'd seen piled up in my fireplace when we were dating, it stung. And when he admired the fact of who I'd become, given my history and my family background, I was reminded of my inferior heritage. His father had been a respected missionary and later a college professor. Mine had been—during his final years, at least—a mentally ill street person.

Having been a single dad for the past six years, Dave cared about the art of homemaking. Keen to please, I began using place mats and napkins at breakfast, especially when his kids were there. I adopted his polite habit of asking each person as they emerged in the morning, "How did you sleep?" (And I learned to answer, "I slept *well*" instead of "I slept *good*.")

I even came around to the idea that dinner should include not just the four major food groups, but the right *colors* (and hopefully one cold dish).

However, when it came to alcohol, the rebel in me rose up. Using Dave's perceived puritanical "judgment" as justification, I began to buy and drink alcohol he didn't know about. At the grocery store, I always bought an extra bottle or two of wine to hide in the garage among the Christmas ornaments. Or I'd stop and get a large beer after taking one of my boys to an afternoon football practice.

At first, it all seemed sort of harmless, something I'd probably admit if Dave asked me. But what began as a sly bit of overindulgence gradually morphed into a secret obsession that took on a life of its own. By the end of our first year of marriage, I had become a sneak, a cheat, and a liar.

In time, I discovered the amazing practicality of four-packs of mini wines, like you get on airplanes. I hid them in my purse, behind books in bookshelves, or tucked inside my tall boots in the closet. I was always on the lookout for new hiding places. (Later, when I met a girl in treatment who hid vodka in her dryer vent, for a second there I was jealous of her creativity.)

As my drinking escalated, so did my tendency to fight with Dave. If he tried to ask me for consideration about how my drinking affected others, in my mind he transformed from a loving, concerned husband into a controlling, oppressive, killjoy. It was impossible for him to mention my drinking gently enough to avoid triggering my shame, which translated instantly into white-hot rage.

In the meantime, I could always find something—money, kids, exes, or a joint work project to feel offended about. We very rarely had blowouts in front of the kids, as per an unspoken agreement we seemed to share. But the kids must have sometimes felt the chill in the air, as arguments often took days to resolve.

Not that Dave didn't try to end them sooner. At first, he made genuine overtures and apologies, which I usually deemed insufficient. Eventually, he began to lose his temper more often, succumbing to outbursts that now strike me as justified. "I'm just a human being!" he'd yell. "And I'm a good husband! But I'm not Jesus! Even Jesus couldn't make you happy!"

He was right. Sometimes, it seemed I couldn't accept anything less than sacrificial demonstrations of love that no man could—or should—give to the best wife on earth, much less one as unreasonable as I was. In retrospect, I had an insatiable need for Dave to show me affection in the face of my most ugly, furious self.

Our marriage became an endless test of his ability to love me at my worst.

One night, when the kids were at our respective exes' houses, Dave and I got into a fight because he hadn't been "romantic" lately. Earlier in the day, I'd felt plenty loved. But after I'd been drinking for a couple hours, I became certain he was emotionally distant. I began to badger him about his not pursuing me like he used to. (As if he could be bullied into whispering sweet nothings!)

The fight escalated when Dave told me my insecurities were "unattractive." The only way I could see to sufficiently express my outrage was to make a dramatic exit. *That'll show him!* I thought, as I grabbed my keys, stomped out the door, and drove off in our minivan.

I'd already had plenty to drink, but I stopped and bought a six-pack of 18-ounce Bud Lights. Then I drove down the highway about fifteen miles to a remote, wooded area with lots of back roads and little traffic. This way, when Dave—close to tears and filled with remorse—searched high and low for me, he wouldn't find me.

I drank the beers as I drove, assuring myself they were just beers and I wasn't actually drunk, so it wasn't drunk driving.

Soon, what with all the beer drinking, I needed to use a bathroom. But where was I going to do that out here? The two tiny convenience stores in this area were long closed. The roads were unlit and dark, and I began to feel confused about where I was.

Finally, I decided I would just pull off and tinkle in the bushes. In the dark, I didn't see the big ditch that bordered the shoulder of the road. Within seconds, I was stuck. I tried everything, including Reverse, gunning it, and twisting the wheel all over. I only managed to dig the van in deeper.

It was winter, and soon I was freezing. I had no cell phone in those days. So after I emptied my bladder in the woods, I turned off the car, worried I'd run out of gas.

For the next hour or so, I sat in the driver's seat and drank my beers as I shivered and wept and felt terribly sorry for myself. My only source of comfort was imagining how Dave would be pacing with panic, or else looking all over town for me, frantic with worry.

I woke up to a knock on my window. The sun had come up, and a policeman stood outside. I turned the key to start the battery and lowered the window. I smiled, trying to appear glad to see a cop, grateful he'd finally shown up. I explained to him I'd gone for a drive, then I'd pulled off the road and hadn't seen the ditch.

"How could you not see such a big ditch?" he asked. "Were you drinking, ma'am?"

"Oh, my gosh! No! Of course not!" I exclaimed, as if horrified by the mere thought. Meanwhile, it occurred to me I had no idea where the empty beer cans from last night were, and I was desperate to make sure he didn't go snooping.

I quickly volunteered that my husband and I both worked for the Christian publisher in town, hoping the information would recast me in the proper light. Everyone knew that only good, God-fearing Christians worked there—people unlikely to be drinking and driving on a dark stretch of road at night.

It worked. His whole demeanor changed. While he went back to his car to call a tow truck, I thanked God for tinted windows and hurriedly gathered up the beer cans from behind my seat, wedged them into a paper bag, and stuffed them under the far back bench of the van where they could now be claimed as empty cans waiting to be returned for the five-cent deposit.

When I got home and explained to Dave what had happened—minus the part about the beers—he didn't seem surprised. And he didn't seem relieved, either.

All he said was, "What were you thinking?"

I wasn't.

⑤

People have asked how Dave could not see what was happening right in front of him? Was he in some kind of deep denial?

I think the answer is yes and no. Yes, he never once found an empty bottle hidden behind a bookshelf or hidden in my boots; he never discovered the stomped-thin beer can stashes I used to keep hidden in the empty space beneath my dresser; he never noticed that my purse weighed ten pounds.

However, he *didn't* miss the fact that I had a major drinking problem and was almost surely an alcoholic. He was keenly aware that I drank way too much. He just didn't know *how* much. Bottom line: *It didn't occur to Dave I might be a secret drunk because he already knew I was a regular drunk.*

From time to time, Dave would notice something was off. He'd wonder aloud, "Why did it seem like you were drunk last night? Didn't you only have a few glasses of wine over the course of a few hours?"

In response, I'd joke about being a lightweight. Or I'd explain I hadn't eaten enough that day, or I'd suggest that maybe the alcohol had mixed badly with my antidepressant.

Dave is by nature not a suspicious person, so he bought my excuses. But even if he hadn't, I was confident that he'd never stoop so low as to search my closet or try to catch me in a lie. That kind of behavior would simply be beneath him. I couldn't even picture it.

Not surprisingly, Dave felt a disconnect between his teetotaler, Christian upbringing and our lifestyle of nightly drinking. He frequently reminded me that he rarely drank in his first marriage, and our lives were veering in a direction he didn't "believe in." Every so often, he'd say, "I know! Let's both quit drinking. Let's see if that wouldn't make for a better life."

"Go for it," I'd tell him. "No one says you have to drink just because I do. What's wrong? Don't you think you can quit by yourself?"

On occasion, Dave would do just that. He'd give up his glass of wine after work or with dinner; he'd stop having a beer on the weekend. He'd go for weeks, hoping it might inspire me to join him. Instead, I'd work hard to wheedle him back into his regular drinking patterns: "Let's take a bottle of wine to the river for a picnic!"

But here's what boggles my mind now. During all those years of drinking, I continued to write and edit Christian books. Publicly, I held forth on things like parenting and prayer, while privately I drank myself past sensibility.

For a long time, Dave and I worked together on a seemingly endless series of projects for a high-profile author who wanted to save the world. At night, I guzzled enormous cans of Bud Light and blamed the author for driving me to drink. I often joked that if I ever had to go to rehab, he should pay the tab.

Ironically, instead of being a source of hope, my Christian background only increased my sense of hopelessness. On the one hand, I knew I was a phony, a hypocrite, and a liar. But on the other hand, I was convinced I'd experienced a genuine conversion to Christ in my teens. Where do you turn for hope when you already have the answer, but it isn't working?

If you're like me, you grow increasingly disillusioned and cynical about your faith. You blame the particular brand of Christianity you've been buying like cereal for years. You judge others for doing exactly what *you* do. And finally, you decide you're just too groovy for any version of the Christian faith that doesn't allow you to indulge in your addiction.

So it went. Through vacations, business travel, funerals, sickness, family reunions, all of our kids' high school graduations, and camping trips—I made it my mission to never be without alcohol. Even if I had to drink in the bathroom stall at Macy's while shopping with my sister, in twelve years I never missed a night of drinking.

And then, just when I thought my drinking couldn't possibly get any worse, it did.

• three •

A BLACKOUT BOTTOM

While I was panicking in Kmart, Dave's interviews at the company were going well.

The next day, we drove around Colorado Springs to look at houses. We both fell in love with the first one we saw, which we'd gotten out of the car to look at through the windows. Dave loved the location—an old-fashioned neighborhood set among huge shade trees where most of the houses were built in the 1890s.

I loved the house's location, too—once I got online and saw it was near not just one but three liquor stores. *Maybe this could work.*

And who knew? Maybe it could be a good thing for me. What if the high elevation helped me to drink less? What if the claustrophobia of our tiny Central Oregon town was the real cause of my need to consume bathtubs of Chardonnay?

We moved to Colorado Springs in early November 2006. At first, I felt hopeful. I loved the view of Pikes Peak, and Dave and I often reminded each other how grateful we should be to move from one mountain paradise to another.

But this paradise, I quickly realized, was an illusion. Not because of God's handiwork, but because he lets people like me loose in it.

After only a few months, I noticed I was drinking even more, not less. And something about it felt worse, not better. Having hoped to make a fresh start, it was somehow even more devastating to find myself painting this fresh white canvas with the same black colors of alcohol, secrecy, and lies.

But it was worse than that, too. Before we moved I'd begun to experience regular blackouts. At the time, I didn't even know this term. I understood passing out, because I did it nightly. It was the reason I usually got in my jammies and went to bed earlier than Dave. I didn't want him to find me clothed, unconscious, and somewhere other than bed, making it obvious I hadn't intentionally fallen asleep.

Blackouts were different. A blackout meant that I would get so drunk at night that even though I appeared conscious and functional, I'd wake up the following morning unable to recall events from the previous evening. Sometimes I could remember bits and pieces. Other times, I could watch a movie with Dave in the evening and the next day watch the same movie alone, *as if I'd never seen it before.*

Not only did these blackouts scare me, they became increasingly hard to hide. One night, my youngest son, Nathan, called me from his Christian college in southern California. I was so excited to finally hear from him. "Nathan! I'm so glad you called," I exclaimed. "I haven't talked to you for weeks!"

He sighed and kind of laughed. "Mom?"

"Yeah?"

"You called me two nights ago and we talked for over an hour."

"Oh yeah!" I said, chuckling nervously. I pressed the phone to my ear, willing myself to recall our conversation. How had Nathan said his classes were going? How was it going with his girlfriend?

There were so many things I wanted to ask my youngest son but couldn't, for fear he'd already told me the answer.

Desperate to avoid these mortifying incidents, every day I sternly reminded myself: *Never pick up the phone after seven o'clock at night! Never go anywhere in your car after dinner!* But clearly, my drunken self couldn't have cared less what my sober self had decided only hours before. At times, I felt like she was out to sabotage me.

Then I watched *Memento*, a movie about a man who suffers from short-term memory loss and writes notes to himself all over his body. Inspired to take a page from the movie, I began to scrawl notes to myself in a journal at night while I was drinking. The next day I'd consult my scribbles so I could pretend to Dave that I remembered what we did last night.

A typical entry might read: "8 wlk Ed w/ D. 9. me L &O. No fgt. D tk Taylor. Me to b 11." (If you don't follow this, it's probably a good sign.)

Sometimes the system broke down. In the morning I couldn't find the new secret place I'd hid my journal while drunk. Or I couldn't make out what the wobbly writing meant. Or I'd gotten too drunk too quickly to write anything.

Once, just after we moved to the Springs, I woke up in the morning and read an entry that made my heart sink. All it said was: "Oh no! Dave broke back in!"

What? I thought with alarm. *Broke back in from where?*

I had no clue.

Later, I learned from Dave that he'd gotten into the hot tub without me because he thought I'd already gone to bed. Angry that he hadn't invited me to join him, I'd gone into a drunken rage and locked him out of the house. Naked.

Fortunately, I was too drunk to remember to lock both the back *and* the front doors (and he had a towel).

Around this same time, we were planning a trip to LA to see my son Nathan, as well as Susan and Larry. I found myself puzzling again over Susan's bizarre abstinence. Since Larry obviously drank, it didn't seem likely that she had a religious objection to alcohol. She didn't strike me as a teetotaler. Heck, she was an actress living in LA. So what was the deal?

Amazingly, it didn't occur to me that Susan might be an alcoholic. I still had a certain image in mind of what an alcoholic looked like. It wasn't me, and it wasn't Susan, either. She was way too put together and decidedly Christian. Most telling of all, she hadn't seemed the slightest bit bothered by the rest of us drinking during that first visit.

I would have been frantic, white-knuckled, and miserable. Clearly, Susan and I had different problems.

Finally, my curiosity got the best of me. On impulse one day, I sent Susan a brief e-mail. Carefully tucked within the casual chit-chat was my real reason for writing: "By the way. I just happened to notice… Why do you not drink?"

A couple days later, Susan replied. "I'm an alcoholic," she wrote. "I go to 12-step meetings."

I was aghast. *Was she talking about those weird clubs where scummy people drink weak coffee and clap a lot?* I couldn't picture Susan doing that. And how could she just admit to being an alcoholic? I cringed, embarrassed on her behalf.

Surely, I thought, *there has to be another way.* God couldn't possibly expect me to seek outside help, or go to those silly meetings. I wasn't like those people. I was a Christian, after all. I was supposed to have victory in Jesus. *What would people think?*

One day, as I was frantically rushing to burn a liquor store box in the fireplace before Dave got home, I started to cry. Staring into the flames, poking at the pieces that wouldn't burn, my panic growing, I remember thinking, *How much longer can I go on like this?*

But I knew better than to think I could just stop. Once again, as I had so many times before, I begged God for a miracle. I reasoned with Him that if He was out there, if He had created the entire universe, He could make me so that I wasn't an alcoholic. If He loved me, He could heal me, fix me. He could do it.

But the miracle never came.

Until one day, weeks later, it did. Only it didn't arrive like I hoped it would, in the form of dramatic rescue. It came in the form of utter, agonizing defeat.

It had been about a month since I got Susan's surprising answer to my e-mail. I doubt that I was even consciously thinking about her at the time. And yet, in retrospect, the very fact of her existence—a Christian alcoholic woman who seemed genuinely happy to be sober now—had planted in me some small seed of hope which, given enough time and misery, began to crack open my heart.

The morning began like any other. As usual, I couldn't remember the events of the previous evening. In the bathroom, my hands shook so much I could hardly get my contacts in my eyes. I worried I'd had yet another ugly fight with Dave the night before. I was vaguely terrified and sick with regret. But what was new about that?

I hadn't been up for more than a half hour when I found myself on my knees by my bed, sobbing violently. I don't remember what I prayed or if it even involved words. All I know is that I was wailing as if one of my sons had died. I was incoherent with despair, pleading for God to help in a way that made all my previous attempts at surrender seem paltry and halfhearted.

I'm not sure how long this went on. But eventually, I got up off the floor. I felt strangely calm. I blew my nose. I think I washed my face. I walked my dog, Edmund, around the block. I drank my coffee while I did some research on the Internet. And then, I called our insurance company to inquire about coverage for alcohol treatment.

ॐ

Later that same afternoon, at around four o'clock, I was devastated to find myself drinking several mini wines from my stash. I had hoped the morning's dramatic episode of surrender meant I might never drink again.

Now, as the wine slid down my throat, it was clear to me I had not magically acquired the ability to stop drinking on my own. What I had acquired was the willingness to lay down my pride and ask for help.

Which in retrospect might have been the greater miracle.

As was my habit, around five o'clock, I opened a bottle of wine from the fridge and poured a little in my glass so when Dave got home and tasted wine on my breath I could motion toward the kitchen and say in all honesty, "I just opened a bottle."

But everything else about this afternoon was different. After all these years of hiding and lying, I was planning to tell Dave the truth about my drinking. An idea that filled me with terror. Not because I was afraid of Dave's reaction, but because I knew that once he knew the truth, it was all over. One way or another, I was going to lose something I couldn't imagine living without.

While I waited for Dave, I reminded myself I didn't have to tell him the *whole* truth all at once. That would be downright mean. I could admit I might have lied to him on occasion (*every day*). That it was quite possible I might have blacked out a time or two (*hundred*). That I may have pilfered a wee bit of our money (*thousands of dollars over twelve years*) to keep my secret stash stocked.

Eventually, Edmund, who would vigilantly keep watch out the

window for Dave's red car at that time of day so he could yelp with ecstasy (conveniently alerting me to Dave's arrival in case I needed to hide something), began his wild barking.

I greeted Dave at the door, hugged him, and asked how his day went.

"It was a crazy day," he said.

"Tell me about your crazy day," I said, summoning false cheer.

But right away, he could tell by my face that something was up. "What's wrong?" he asked. "You look so serious. Have you been crying?"

"I was crying a lot this morning," I admitted.

"Talk to me," he said.

"I do need to talk to you. Why don't we get some wine first? I just opened a bottle." (I wanted him to have wine in his hand while I made my confession, since it might remind him to feel at least a little culpable himself.)

While Dave poured us glasses in the kitchen, I settled on our leather couch in the living room and tried to look meek. In classic manipulation mode, I had already thought about how I should appear and sound and seem as I told him the truth. I hoped I would cry. I was afraid I wouldn't.

He sat down and waited. The irony of the glasses in our hands didn't escape me. I gulped from mine. Sighed deeply. When I couldn't seem to get started talking, Dave got irritated. "Come on. What is it? You're scaring me."

"I'm sorry," I said nervously. He was right, though. There's nothing worse than when your spouse seems about to say something momentous and can't seem to get it out. Your mind goes to the worst places.

"Okay," I finally said, hugging a throw pillow to my chest. "I guess I wanted to tell you that I think my drinking problem might be even worse than you think."

"What do you mean?" he asked, probably thinking I didn't realize how bad he already thought it was.

"I drink more than you know about, I think." I could feel my face go flush.

He looked at me with surprise. "Do you mean you drink in secret?"

"Well," I said thoughtfully, as if trying hard to recall such an occasion, "I guess I have in the past." (Last night counts as the past, right?)

"Okay," he said, looking confused. He set his wine on the coffee table. But before he could ask more questions, ones that might lead to the topics of lying and secrets, I impulsively charged ahead. "I think I need to go somewhere to get help."

"Okay," he said again, nodding, taking this in with his trademark calm.

"I can't stop drinking!" I blurted. And to my surprise, something about hearing myself say this out loud, after so many years of pretending I could stop whenever I wanted to, opened the floodgates. I didn't even have to *try* to cry.

"Oh, honey," Dave said. He pulled me into his arms and that made me cry even more. He rocked me just a little. "I think you should go to treatment right away," he said. "It's going to be okay."

I could feel his lips on my wet hair on my cheek as he comforted me. I could feel Edmund watching us from the floor, jealous.

As Dave repeated in my ear, "It's going to be okay," I realized he was saying it to himself as much as to me. When I pulled away to look at him, he said, "As soon as possible, honey. Treatment. How about I take you tomorrow?"

Things weren't unfolding how I'd pictured. I'd been so worked up about this, so prepared for him to grill me for details: *How much was I drinking? When and where had I hidden alcohol? How long had I been lying to him?*

Now I realized this was how *I* would have reacted under similar circumstances. I should have known Dave's reaction would be concern, quickly followed by eagerness to "fix" this thing—get me into treatment—before I changed my mind. He's a smart man. He knew there'd be plenty of time later for questions or anger. (Which there was.)

I went to the bathroom and blew my nose. When I sat back down, I reminded him there was a problem so far as the *timing* of treatment. Our nephew Adam was getting married in two weeks. It was going to be a huge family affair in LA, and my sister, Katherine, was counting on us. If I checked into some kind of treatment program now, I'd miss the wedding.

Even as I laid out the problem, I could see Dave getting agitated. "You shouldn't put this off," he said.

"But I have a solution!" I told him. I quickly explained I'd already called the insurance company and I'd found a treatment facility in Pueblo (an hour south of home). I could schedule myself for admission on the Tuesday following the wedding. And since we'd be seeing my kids and a lot of our relatives there, I could plan to tell everyone at once that I was going to treatment.

"I think that's a terrible plan," Dave declared. "Why don't you just *wait* to tell people until *after* you go? Why say what you're going to do before you even do it?"

"But that's exactly the point," I countered. "If everyone knows I'm going to treatment and that I have a problem, it will be almost impossible for me to change my mind."

Having no real alternative, Dave finally agreed to the plan.

Later, I realized he was probably more than a little embarrassed by the whole prospect. And I don't blame him. If your wife announces to everyone that, oh, by the way, she's a raging drunk and has been hiding it for a dozen years, what does that say about her husband?

• four •

TOASTING THE TRUTH

In the days following my confession, I continued to unfold some of my secrets to Dave, one small corner at a time. I told him about my secret stash, the wine in my closet right now, the surreptitious trips to the liquor store, the weekly bottle hunt on garbage day for all the empties, the almost nightly black-outs...

Naturally, Dave had questions:

"You mean you drank in the ladies room when we were out to dinner?"

"Yes," I said, leaving off the embarrassing tidbit that I put the empties in the sanitary napkin dispenser.

"And when you went to sleep so early, it wasn't just your antide-pressants?"

"I think they call it passing out."

At some point, he said, "You fell down a lot."

What? "I was falling down?" I didn't realize this. He said that ever since we moved to the Springs, I stumbled a lot at night.

In yet another conversation, we got to a question of his I'd been dreading: "What about sex? When we made love, could you even remember it the next day?"

"Sometimes," I told him, which was barely true. "But hey," I added with false cheer, "I remember every time when we did it in the morning!" (almost never).

The details came in jerks and starts. At times, I felt as though I was disclosing the painful revelations of an extramarital affair. And in a way, I was. When you consider how thoroughly I had betrayed Dave's trust, how frequently I had lied to his face, and how deliberately deceitful I'd been—it was very much as if alcohol had been my secret lover.

But here's the strange part. After my confession, during the two weeks leading up to my nephew's wedding, nothing changed. Even as Dave and I discussed plans for my entering treatment, I couldn't bring myself to drink in front of him the ridiculous amounts of alcohol that my body still required. So I continued to drink in secret.

And Dave never asked. I think he understood I couldn't stop drinking copious amounts of alcohol, and he was kind enough to look away and grant me a smidgen of dignity.

We did agree that *after* Pueblo, we'd *both* quit drinking. But only one of us was truly enthused about this prospect. All I had to do was remember any number of excruciating evenings when I'd tried—and failed—to not drink for just one night. Why wouldn't a whole string of such nights amount to torture?

Every day, I anticipated my future suffering like a person doomed to hell. But even people bound for hell sometimes wonder how hot it will get there.

I wanted a preview. One day, I told Dave I had gotten online and found a recovery meeting I wanted to try out. I was pretty sure that after treatment these meetings were going to be part of my new life.

What happened next will forever stand as one of the kindest things my husband has ever done for me. He offered to go with me.

§

At the time, I thought he was just being nice. Now I know it was a sign of how deeply he planned to invest in my recovery, and an indicator of how close I had come to losing him.

A little before noon on the following Sunday, we pulled up in the parking lot of a large metal building that looked like a storage facility or a car repair shop. Neither of us moved to leave the car. "I'm not sure I could have done this without you," I told Dave sincerely, wiping my sweaty hands on the legs of my jeans.

"You owe me big-time," he agreed, taking a deep breath.

His admission surprised me. As a general rule, Dave is undaunted by potentially awkward social situations. He tends to dawdle and be polite while I get anxious to make a quick exit. Now, I thought he looked a little green around the gills, which I found strangely gratifying. Maybe for once he'd be as ready as I always was to bolt for the door.

During the short drive over, I had planned the whole thing out. How we'd sit in the back of the room and be invisible. How I would listen without speaking and decide if I ever wanted to come back here alone. How, after the meeting, we'd both slip out before anyone had a chance to nab us and do to us whatever it was they did to new people.

As soon as we walked into the barnlike room, my master plan went to pieces. (Never trust ideas you get from TV.) For one thing, there was no "back of the room." And no crowd to get lost in, either. There were just five middle-aged men and one woman gathered around a cafeteria-style table.

And all eyes were on us.

As we took our seats, I could feel my face turn pink and my limbs go numb. Glancing around the room in an effort to avoid the curious gazes of these strangers, I noticed numerous plaques on the walls. They sported obvious clichés, like "Live and let live" and "Take it easy."

As a writer, I knew this didn't bode well.

Next thing I knew, one of the men was handing Dave a plastic sheet with text. "Would you mind reading this when it's time?" he asked.

Dave said he would. But I could feel his nervousness. Was this how they treated newcomers? Part of me wanted to speak up and explain that Dave was here with me (innocent, in other words). He shouldn't have to read! But I was so stricken with embarrassment to be here that my mouth wouldn't work.

A man with a ponytail opened the meeting with a short, cloying prayer about serenity. Then, while my hands trembled in my lap, Dave read some kind of introduction. After he was done, we went around the table and introduced ourselves. I was expecting this part (TV again). I also knew they would say, "I'm So-and-So and I'm an alcoholic."

I also knew that we *wouldn't* be saying that. But what were we supposed to say instead? Why hadn't I planned ahead? I wondered how long it might take me—months, years, if ever?—before I could say those shameful words in public, much less in front of Dave, and much more less in front of strangers.

To my relief, the introductions came around to Dave first before they got to me. He said something mature, but noncommittal, like, "I'm Dave, and I'm here with my wife, Heather. I think we might have some drinking issues."

Then it was my turn. My face burned. I had sternly promised myself I would *not* cry in this meeting, and yet to my horror, tears sprang to my eyes. When I opened my mouth to say my name, the truth came out instead: "I'm Heather and I'm an alcoholic."

More tears, a veritable gushing.

Someone casually scooted a box of tissues down the table, as if bawling was par for the course.

After the leader talked for about ten minutes, each person around the table shared. When it was my turn, I wiped my eyes and haltingly explained that *I* was the alcoholic, not my husband. I don't know what else I said, but when the group realized that this was my first ever meeting—not just my first time to this particular meeting—they exclaimed in great surprise, as if I was a celebrity they hadn't recognized.

Then and there, the leader called for the chip tray and took out a plastic coin. He explained that it was a newcomer chip, and I should take it if I had a desire to stop drinking. I took the coin, along with a hug from the man. (The way he stood up and came at me, I got the feeling it was mandatory.)

When the meeting was over, Dave and I followed everyone's lead as we all formed a circle and held hands, like children on a playground getting ready to play Duck Duck Goose. And once again, the Serenity Prayer. The word *serene* made me think of a bubble bath commercial featuring a woman floating in a mountain of foam. *Except in real life, she would have a glass of wine nearby,* I thought.

After we let go of hands, but before we could dash for the door, the only other woman there rushed over and introduced herself. She pulled from her purse a schedule of meetings around town and began to circle the ones she thought I'd like.

I nodded, pretending enthusiasm. Finally, she wrote her phone number on the schedule and urged me to call her.

Why would I call her? To say what? I'd just met her!

That was when I noticed that the guy wearing a long ponytail—the same one who had given me the chip—had us cornered, too. Grinning like a TV preacher, he handed me a big blue paperback book that looked a little like a Bible. He said it had been written by another drunk, and if I read it, it would help me to stay sober.

Embarrassed, I tried to resist. "I'll order one online!" I promised.

But he insisted I shouldn't wait. Like it was an emergency.

When I got home and flipped through the huge paperback, I saw where the man had carefully highlighted many passages in yellow. It tugged a bit at my heart to think of this burly guy with dirty fingernails combing this text for hope.

〜

Since Nathan was already at college in LA, Dave and I flew there the day before my nephew's wedding. After meeting Noah at LAX, we picked up Nathan from his school, and the four of us drove out to the Santa Monica Pier for lunch. I wanted to talk to both my boys together about my plans.

I still cringe when I remember the scene. There I was, sitting at an outdoor Mexican restaurant under a brightly colored umbrella, sipping hard on a Heineken while I explained to my beautiful sons that I had a serious problem with alcohol.

"You guys already know I was a nightly drinker," I acknowledged. "I mean, every night by five…"

They nodded while I tipped my green bottle and gulped. Wiped my mouth. "But what you don't know is that I think I have a real problem with alcohol. And for many years now, I've been hiding how much I drank." This got their attention.

I took another draw on my Heineken, savoring the crisp, malty taste on my tongue. "After tomorrow's wedding," I continued, "when Dave and I get back to Colorado, I'm going to enter treatment."

In the brief silence that followed, I watched Noah squint at me with one eye shut against the glare of the California sun. Was that an accusing look? They both had every right to be upset with me. All through their high school years, I'd always come down hard on them about occasional incidents involving drinking or dope.

In Nathan's case, these had seemed like normal teenage experimentation. He'd been my easy child—good-humored, friendly, and outgoing. I thought of him as my "shiny" boy because he was blond and fair and kind and good. When I watched his college debate competitions, I could always tell that even if the other team scored more points, Nathan was the guy people wanted to *vote* for.

Noah, three years older than Nathan, was in many ways his brother's opposite. He was dark-haired, impossibly tall, introverted, and incurably moody. Noah was no less loved, smart, or talented than his brother. He had a great gift for music and a photographic memory, and he was the guy you didn't want to challenge to a game of Boggle.

But in recent years, as Nathan set his sights on sports, girls, and getting into law school, Noah had turned to drugs and alcohol. While Nathan made me feel like the best mom on the planet, I was pretty sure I'd screwed up Noah's life irreparably. Having given up on college, he struggled just to live and keep a job.

By now, Noah's own problems with alcohol and drugs were well established. A few years earlier, all four of us parents had become so worried about him that we staged a mini intervention at his apartment in Eugene, Oregon. Undaunted by the fact that my own purse was loaded with small bottles of wine, I had joined the parental chorus urging Noah to get the help he so clearly needed.

Today, it's hard to comprehend my hypocrisy, except to say that I was so deeply lost in my own nightmare that I was genuinely desperate to save my son from a similar fate—even as I blindly led the way.

The intervention with Noah failed. He completed a three-month program in California, and then he drank on his first night out.

After that, Noah took a couple more brief stabs at sobriety. But for the most part, he continued to spiral even more deeply into alcoholism and severe depression. I'd love to tell you I spent all those years lying awake in the middle of the night waiting for the proverbial dreaded phone call—except that wouldn't be true, since most nights I was passed out by eleven...

Now, my Heineken already gone, I braced for the worst. What if Noah got so angry at me for lying about my drinking that he went out and did something dumb? What if my admission sent him into an even darker place? What if I was doomed to watch my son continue to slowly kill himself with no way to numb my own pain? (See, even then, I was thinking about *me*.)

My guilty conscience told me it would serve me right. Thousands of perfectly good and kind and sober mothers who didn't deserve to lose their sons had watched them die that way. Why should I escape such a fate when I'd set such a bad example for so many years?

But the angry recriminations or accusing questions from my sons never came—at least not on that pier in Santa Monica. Instead, Noah was skeptical. "You don't have enough good stories, Mom," he said. "If you go to rehab, you're going to suck. You're going to be in there with a bunch of losers my age. And besides, I don't think you can stop drinking."

Thanks for your support, Son.

Nathan (whom I'd recently forgotten an entire conversation with) was a bit more reflective. "Wow. That's great, Mom," he said. "Good for you."

As we continued to discuss my gradual descent into alcoholism, I ordered another Heineken, and both boys ordered jumbo margaritas, each the size of a small mixing bowl. I wondered if maybe this was what people meant when they talked about entire families being in denial.

§

The following afternoon, so as not to detract from the joyous occasion, I waited until after my nephew's wedding ceremony and well into the reception before I began to blab my news. Fortified by ample quantities of wine, I casually worked the round tables. I spoke to friends, relatives, and even ex-relatives, whispering, "I just wanted you to know I have a drinking problem. I'm going somewhere for help…"

In some cases I was greeted by mild surprise. In a few cases, there were tears of relief. In no instance was anyone noticeably shocked. Obviously, my secret wasn't as big of a secret as I'd thought.

Or maybe…maybe I was simply overstating things, exaggerating my problem! That must be it. What if I didn't need to go to treatment after all?!

But my alcohol-soaked revelation had come too late. By now, I'd already announced my news to the world. I had accomplished what I wanted—and backed myself into a corner. Chagrined, I knew that from now on everyone would be watching me at family get-togethers, wondering how I was doing in my quest to get sober.

By the time the reception was over, I was giddy with relief. And weak with dread.

five

PANIC IN PUEBLO

O n Tuesday morning, April 3, 2007, I got up, showered, and packed a suitcase for treatment. I knew from TV (this part also turned out to be true), that someone would search my bags, so I didn't bother trying to smuggle in alcohol. However, I did pack a new bathrobe, on the weird off chance that where I was going it might be part of my public attire (I was correct on this).

Dave had offered, as I knew he would, to take the morning off work and drive me down to Pueblo. But I'd declined. If I went alone, I could still bail at the last minute. And if I didn't end up bailing, then at least the decision to get help would be wholly mine.

Around nine a.m., I got in my car and headed south on the freeway. The closer I got to Pueblo, the more ludicrous the whole idea seemed. Of course, I wasn't going to voluntarily enter my personal version of hell! So why was I still driving south?

With each mile, I felt more frantic. I began to pray I'd get into an accident, break down by the road, or be taken in the Rapture.

41

Meanwhile, I kept a keen eye out for hitchhikers, in case I could pick up a homicidal maniac.

When disaster failed to materialize, I arrived on Club Manor Drive (was this an intentional joke?) in front of an innocuous building. It looked nothing like a place where drunks were tortured into dryness. I turned off the ignition and sat there. All I could think was, *Why didn't I bring any wine?* I wanted to kick myself. I had blown my last chance to say a proper, last-minute farewell to Chardonnay.

Plus, I knew this facility's program was voluntary. You could leave at any time. There'd be no fences or bars. What if I bolted? What if I ran out of the building crying and screaming that I had to have wine?

I could easily picture this.

I gripped my steering wheel and forced the words out of my mouth, "Dear God, save me. I just can't do this! Help me!"

Nothing happened. No angels descended. But after a few minutes, I was surprised to find myself in motion. In a surreal daze, I pulled my luggage from the back of my car and rolled my bag and myself through the front doors.

After a brief meeting with the woman in charge of admissions, she handed me off to a sweet-faced, heavyset nurse named Bonnie. Bonnie chatted jovially with me, then whisked me into a small room to give me a Breathalyzer test. She was so tender about it that I felt like a child getting my temperature taken.

So far, so good.

When she told me I still had a good amount of alcohol in my system, I was surprised: *How many times had I woken up drunk from the night before—and not known it?*

The previous evening, Dave had made me a "last supper" of halibut, saffron rice, and asparagus, accompanied by a bottle of my favorite Chardonnay.

But now it suddenly occurred to me that I hadn't relished my last drink. I should have savored the moment, or at least drank from a beautiful glass. But instead, shame made me take my last drink where I'd guzzled so many before—on the toilet in my bathroom with the door locked.

After I had surrendered my bag for inspection, Bonnie led me to the main living area, where couches were arranged in a large U shape facing a television against one wall (used only for outdated instructional videos, it turned out). But the main thing I noticed was the smell. *Why did it smell like popcorn?*

Then Bonnie gave me a tour of the small kitchen (used only for snacks), situated right off the living area, and I saw it—a commercial-sized popcorn maker. I thought of my son Noah. He would be in heaven here. He's the only person I know who has ever stopped by a cinema to buy popcorn *without* going to any movie. Who does that?

Now, sometimes, I'll be in the foyer of a movie theater and the buttery aroma of popcorn will hit me, and in a flash I'm back in that small kitchen, terror nipping at my heels, readying myself to meet a random group of complete strangers—each of whom, like it or not, will play an important role in my recovery.

๑

In typical, self-centered fashion, I had imagined that treatment would be all about me. I had pictured myself spending a lot of one-on-one time with the staff psychiatrist while he probed my psyche to solve the mystery of what drove someone as nice as me to drink myself blotto. Sure, I knew the other patients would be there, hovering in the background.

But in my mind, the camera was always focused on me, front and center.

It was nothing like that.

I quickly learned that rehab is nothing if not a group activity. It's like one long experiment in the study of how people develop intimacy with strangers. Naturally, whether or not this is a good thing depends largely on who your fellow residents happen to be. These are the people who will see you with bed-head at six a.m. when you stumble half asleep down the hall to have your vitals taken. Who will learn your most shameful secrets. Who will see you exposed for what you are—a blubbering drunk in Banana Republic clothes.

Who won't like you.

It was true. Right away, several of the residents decided I thought I was better than them. During dinner in the school-style cafeteria that first night, a lesbian and meth addict named Geneva mocked me for being so "put together." She said I looked like one of the damn counselors. She was sure if I met her on the street, I wouldn't give her the f*@*#ing time of day.

Others at the table nodded or snickered.

I had half-expected this—not quite fitting in. But I was taken aback by the open hostility. I went to my room and cried. What did these people want from me? Should I not put on makeup and blow-dry my hair? Should I wear only T-shirts? Forgive me for not knowing what a "tweaker" is! (It's a methamphetamine addict.) *I don't think I'm* better *than any of them!* I insisted to myself.

And yet, I did think I was *different*. I just wasn't in the same category as these hard-core alcoholics and drug addicts. I'd never stolen anything. I'd never spent time in jail or on the street. I'd never woken up naked in Vegas, unsure how I got there and who was in bed with me.

That night, I phoned Dave and told him I'd met a drug-addicted lesbian named Geneva who hated me on sight. I told him I missed him. I missed Edmund. I missed being at home in our house on our wide, pretty street where no one ever looked at me funny, wore pajamas to dinner, or asked me what I was "in for."

ৎ

Before I came to treatment, I envisioned myself here curled up in a corner, sweating profusely, delirious with pain, and perhaps suffering small seizures. But that never happened. Much to my relief, during those first couple days, I was given Valium to help me cope with the physical symptoms of withdrawal.

In the meantime, because I was new and detoxing, I was temporarily excused from most of the program activities. Since I didn't have a roommate, this allowed me plenty of time to wallow in self-pity. In fact, I was so worried about being ostracized that I forgot to worry about not being able to drink.

At around eight on that first night, the irony hit me. Instead of climbing the walls with craving as I'd expected, I was alone in my room, calmly reading a book, desperately upset because a lesbian didn't like me.

Obviously, I had worried about all the wrong things.

ৎ

By the third day, after being tapered off the Valium, I was expected to fully participate in the schedule of the program. It was time to join my group—the other half-dozen or so people who were also in their first week. These were the folks with whom I would attend most classes and take field trips (bowling).

It didn't take me long to gravitate toward a couple women who seemed safer than Geneva. Sure, I was a bit older, and I didn't necessarily share their family or socioeconomic background. But

I decided to make a concerted effort to be friendly. Not just with them, but everyone.

Uninvited, I began to join small groups of people who gathered out on the back patio during breaks between classes to smoke and talk. I asked about their lives and families. I looked at wallet-sized photos of kids who, in most cases, were no longer in their parent's custody.

When I could, I added my own lame stories. I told them about the time my husband and I were out to dinner with friends and I had drunk too much and I sat on a toilet in a public restroom and tinkled with great relief only to realize that something warm was happening, that this toilet had a lid—and the lid was down, and I was sitting on it.

Their laughter was reassuring.

Around the fourth day of my stay, I sensed that something had shifted. Most, if not all, of the other patients had accepted me.

A girl in her early twenties named Robin, who seemed way too sweet to be a heroin addict, began to sit by me whenever we gathered as a group. Sometimes she'd lay her head on my shoulder. Robin had red hair and the creamiest white skin. She told me how she'd lost her fiancé in a motorcycle accident. It had been her idea to go without helmets, and now she couldn't deal with the guilt.

One day, I was talking to a guy named Bart about his stint in prison. A couple other people who'd also been incarcerated joined the conversation. Listening to their humorous spin on their sad stories, I suddenly realized that this was the closest I'd come to being acquainted with a criminal since the year I donated a gift to a charity tree sponsored by a prison ministry in the mall.

Maybe my life had been a bit sheltered.

Eventually, even Geneva seemed interested in being my friend. One night, as we were sitting on one of the picnic tables chatting, she told me about her nine-year-old daughter. As she opened up to me about being an absent mom, I realized I'd never before (to my knowledge) had an actual conversation with a lesbian, much less tried to open my mind and heart to one.

When Geneva began to jokingly come on to me, I was *way* more relieved than worried. One day, during our morning meeting, it was my turn to read from the inspirational book we always used. Reflexively, I started searching around me on the couch for my reading glasses. A guy named Mike pointed out, "Heather, they're in your shirt."

I looked down. He was right. I often tucked the frames into the V of my top or blouse. As I reached for them, Geneva called out from across the room, "Wait! Let *me* get them for you!"

Everyone laughed. And I knew I was *in*.

ৎ

Now, if only I could get somewhere with the staff psychiatrist. So far, my two brief sessions with him had proved disappointing. When was this guy going to get to the *point*?

He wasn't asking any of the right questions. I was still convinced I needed to uncover the deep-seated, psychological reason I'd become an alcoholic. Could it be something painful from my childhood? My experience of father loss or my stepdad's abuse? The idea made sense, but it seemed like I'd already dealt with that stuff through counseling and prayer in my twenties.

One afternoon, a counselor named Gary told us in class that we didn't drink because of our past, or because of some mysterious mental or emotional hang-up. He acknowledged that lots of addicts with mental issues or troubled histories benefit from therapy. But as to the root cause of our drinking, he urged us to look no further than our vulnerability to the "*disease* called alcoholism."

The word *disease* caught my attention. Hadn't I been warned about that word? I specifically remembered sitting in a Bible study years ago with a group of fellow Christians when the topic of addiction came up. Their blood had boiled at the idea of calling it a disease. If memory served, they'd been adamant that people used this word as an excuse to sin.

My hand went up. "I'm sorry," I said. "But I always heard that calling alcoholism a disease was just a way to not take responsibility. Isn't a disease something that you get through no fault of your own? How can you call it a disease if it could have been avoided had you not participated in a certain behavior?"

Whew! I'm so articulate! I thought. I couldn't wait to see Gary's baffled expression as he struggled to explain himself.

Instead, Gary calmly pointed out that no one would propose that lung cancer directly caused by cigarettes, or diabetes brought on by obesity, are *not* legitimate diseases, even when they arise from or are triggered by an avoidable indulgence. "And like any disease," he added, "alcoholism is progressive. It gets worse over time, never better. Left untreated, it often results in death."

I was momentarily stunned into silence.

"But I'm curious," Gary continued, his eyes resting on me. "What is it about labeling alcoholism a disease that *you* object to so much?"

I hemmed and hawed, red-faced. Finally, I reminded him—and the rest of the class—that I never said *I* thought this way about the word *disease*, only that I'd been *told* this by others.

Later, I brooded over our exchange. A mantra I'd been hearing in treatment came to mind. "We're not bad people getting good, we're sick people getting well." Wasn't this idea at the heart of why some Christians objected to labeling addiction a disease instead of a moral issue?

As long as we defined the *problem* as sin, the *solution* pointed to God. But if the problem was an illness, the solution would point beyond the walls of the church, maybe toward the kind of treatment I was undergoing.

So what did I believe?

Part of me preferred the simplicity and moral clarity of the sin paradigm. It was conveniently cut and dried. But if my alcoholism was purely a sin issue, why couldn't I win the battle? How many times had I repented, begged forgiveness of God, and sworn off drinking—only to fail miserably and drink even more to deal with the guilt?

And yet, I also couldn't say that sin didn't play a part. Of course it did. I sinned every time I hid my drinking, drank to get drunk, or lied to my husband.

The more I thought about it, the more it seemed to me that alcoholism wasn't a matter of sin *or* sickness, but *both*. My own experience had proven to me in a way no theory or doctrine ever could that the issue was much more complicated than a single paradigm could explain.

six

THE SHOCK OF SOBER SEX

On Friday afternoon during that first week in treatment, I stood in front of the admissions director. "You want me to do what?" I asked her. "I don't get it."

"Just come back bright and early Monday morning and we'll check you back in and continue with treatment. And don't drink while you're gone."

I was barely done with detox and I was being encouraged to spend the upcoming weekend at home. The reason had nothing to do with me or my progress or what seemed best for my recovery. It was all about our insurance, which would pay only for a limited number of inpatient nights. Spending a weekend at home would leave me more coverage for weekdays, which was when important classes took place.

I understood. But the idea of going home so soon alarmed me greatly. I didn't feel ready. By now, I understood the idea of "triggers." And I'd also been told repeatedly that we had to dump our old drinking or drugging buddies in favor of new, sober friends. Find new playgrounds, they said.

All fine and good. Except I lived in what had been my bar, and I was married to my drinking buddy, even if half the time he hadn't known how much his buddy was drinking. Just the idea of Dave made me want to drink.

What if he secretly felt the same? Could we find a new way to unwind at five o' clock without popping a cork to reward ourselves for living on the planet another day?

What if I went home and relapsed?

Driving away from Club Manor Drive that Friday afternoon, instead of feeling happy or free, I felt like a convict who'd been released *way* too soon. Every exit on the freeway invited me to turn off, find a liquor store, and prove to everyone that I couldn't do this thing.

Somehow, I arrived back in the Springs safe and sober. And yet, my homecoming was unexpectedly awkward. I felt oddly shy of my husband, who met me at the door and hugged me for a long time. He noticed the couple pounds I'd lost (amazing what eliminating 1,000 calories per day in wine will do) and congratulated me on making it this far. "I'm so proud of you, honey," he kept saying.

One of the first things I did was open the fridge...to no alcohol. Where several bottles of wine would normally be, there was a bottle of dark purple pomegranate juice. Dave cheerily poured some into red wine goblets and we drank them on our enclosed front porch with false bravado. Both of us passed on the strong cheese, which used to go so well with a dark red.

A half hour later, I moved on to sparkling water. Not because I was thirsty, but because I still needed to constantly drink something—*anything*. Or maybe I just needed the familiar motion of lifting a drink to my mouth.

After dinner, both of us feeling at loose ends, we went for a walk. It was a lovely spring evening, but what I remember most about it were the lilacs, which were in bloom early. In Colorado

Springs, they grow so profusely that the lush purple branches crowd sidewalks and hang over back fences. The air smelled so sweet that I felt in a swoon.

While we strolled, I noticed how Dave's hand felt in mine, the weak sun on my face like a balm. Had I missed such details before, or was the whole world new?

Then, as we neared home, I realized that we still had several hours ahead of us before we could reasonably go to bed. What on earth would we *do*? Agitation quickly washed away my calm as it dawned on me that drinking hadn't been only about consuming alcohol. It had been my main activity. It was what I did for what passed as living.

Back at the house, Dave and I both poured ourselves another glass of sparkling water and settled on the couch to watch TV. I tried to stay interested, but the shows weren't nearly as entertaining as when I used to watch them drunk without being able to remember them later.

Now I wondered if Dave had been right all along when he used to tease me about the dumb shows I watched. "So, let me guess," he'd say, passing through the room while I was glued to the TV. "It's a show about bad people doing bad things?"

They always were.

Finally, it was time for bed. I remember feeling elated to brush my teeth and be aware of what I was doing. I was glad to climb in bed with a book knowing I'd be able to recall the storyline in the morning. But how could Dave possibly understand the trepidation I felt about the idea of sober sex?

Toward the end of my drinking, usually the only way I could even know that my husband and I had been together the evening before was if in the morning I found my undies by my bed—a helpful reminder to myself that I should mention to him how much I enjoyed last night.

Now I realized I had learned to rely on alcohol not only to get me in the mood, but to tell me what to do once I got there. With little recall of past specifics, I was left to wonder: What all did we do, and how did we do it? Did I generally make a lot of noise? Or were we more tender and circumspect?

I couldn't say for sure. But my general impression was that toward the end of my drinking, I'd been much more wild, experimental, and unselfconscious in bed.

I didn't let on to Dave how awkward it felt, because I didn't want to remind him how little I remembered of our former lovemaking.

But dear God, he was so naked! I was so naked! And did we *really* have to do it while we were both so wide awake?

Afterward, he said, "I love being with you sober," and I heartily echoed the sentiment. But did he mean it, or was he just being polite? I knew I should ask him, but I was worried that he would say in the kindest possible terms, "You were way more fun in bed when you were drunk."

That night, while I lay there trying to master the trick of falling asleep when you're wide awake, I wished I was already back at treatment. Where I didn't have a husband who was so alarmingly *present*. Where drinking wasn't even an option. Where I didn't have to wonder if I still had some mini wines hidden somewhere inside my closet. Maybe in my winter boots?

I thought about Robin and Geneva and a girl named Nicole, who I knew were planning to break out the board games and eat popcorn that night. I wondered if they missed me. And suddenly I understood why Nicole had once said wistfully: "If only I could just live here forever..."

As I drifted off to sleep, I felt Dave's arm come over my side, his breath at the back of my neck and hair. "Do you think you'll stay sober, Heather?" he whispered.

"I hope so," I told him. "But they say not to promise."

෨

Bright and early Monday morning, I returned with my suitcase, relieved I'd made it through the weekend.

That was when I learned that my insurance wanted me to finish the program, but they wouldn't pay for me to sleep there. Probably, the admissions director knew this was the case on Friday. Now, she explained I should get a room at a nearby hotel. Lots of people did it this way, she said.

But it wasn't as simple as it sounded. That evening, as everyone else headed to bed and lights out, I got in my car and drove over to the discount hotel she'd recommended. Apparently, the treatment center had arranged for their patients to be given a special rate there. Who knew you could get a big discount for being a drunk?

As I dragged my suitcase down the hall to my room, I felt disoriented and scared. I had a car, after all. And no one checking on me. Plus, there was a liquor store nearby. I could easily drink if I wanted to—a farewell glass or two—and no one would ever know.

I reminded myself it wasn't like I was under arrest. I was paying them (the treatment center) to learn about this "disease." Plus, no one had made me swear I would never drink again. In fact, I never said to anyone I wouldn't! Not once. Not even to Dave!

The realization made me want to hoot for joy.

Then, something I'd heard one of the counselors say popped into my mind. She'd explained that alcohol was like an allergy. In the same way some people are allergic to peanuts or strawberries, an alcoholic can't drink alcohol without an abnormal reaction, an insatiable craving for more. Like someone who eats and gets hungry instead of full.

At the time, the idea hadn't seemed revolutionary. Now, I considered it in light of my experience. Wasn't it true that I had *never* in my life thought I'd had enough to drink? Like thirst in reverse,

I always wanted more, not less. I might run out, lose access, suc-
cumb to social pressure, or pass out. But I had never once thought,
Okay, I've had enough. That's better now.

It was this new knowledge—if I drank just one glass, I'd crave a
drink even more than I already did—that stopped me short. Why
would I want to make this harder than it already was? Obviously,
for me there was no such thing as enjoying a couple good-bye
glasses of Chardonnay.

I didn't drink that night. Instead, I began a new routine. Every
evening after the program activities ended at around nine p.m., I
came back to my hotel room and called Dave to report on my day.
Then I'd go down the hall to the vending machines and buy Cheetos and a Diet Coke. I'd get in my nightie and eat my snack in bed
while watching mindless TV shows.

Every morning, I woke up alone in a strange bed with a scratchy
gold cover. I made myself weak hotel coffee and sat by a window
in my room that looked onto the parking lot. I journaled and read
my daily Bible, which I'd brought from home this time. At seven
a.m., I went back to treatment in time to join everyone for rubbery
scrambled eggs. Geneva, Robin, or Nicole usually saved me a seat
at their table.

The days were taken up by classes on addiction, with breaks in
between to give people time to smoke outside, visit, and do home-
work. Most nights, after dinner we piled into a large van and went
to a 12-step meeting somewhere in the town of Pueblo. Occasionally, we had our own evening meeting.

Then, it was back to the hotel for me.

After a while I started to feel like I was living in a strange, alter-
nate universe. *And I kind of liked it.*

seven

DRUNKS LIKE ME

At least once every few days, a new resident arrived. I'd be lounging comfortably on the sofa in the great room next to Robin or Geneva, and I'd look up to see Nurse Bonnie with a new "victim." "Fresh blood," we liked to joke.

He or she almost always looked angry or scared or both. Either way, my heart went out. It was hard to believe that not so long ago that was *me*—standing in the kitchen with Bonnie, inhaling the aroma of popcorn, a lump of fear lodged in my throat.

Now I felt perfectly at home here.

Some of the young male patients who were in their twenties reminded me of Noah. I scanned their faces for some sign that they were really ready to get sober, that Mom or Dad or the taxpayer or whoever was footing this bill wasn't wasting their money.

But most of them just looked bored. I learned that quite a few had been in treatment numerous times before, and this explained the cynicism behind their eyes. Why would rehab work this time when it hadn't before?

I used to feel that way every time I repented of my drinking.

After so many failed attempts to do a U-turn, you begin to doubt your own sincerity.

When I could, I tried to reach out to these young men in an encouraging way. My heart went out to them, but maybe even more so to their moms. I kept thinking, *What if this was Noah?*

Which got me wondering about the time when Noah went to treatment and it hadn't stuck. Had he met moms there like me—whose hearts went out to Noah's poor mother? They probably pictured some nice lady, not a secret drunk who couldn't stop drinking long enough to save her own son.

One day, a new, elderly patient named Helen checked in. With her spectacle glasses and frumpy business clothes, she looked like someone's grandma. And here I'd thought *I* was too old!

Anxious to welcome her, I set aside my Diet Coke and went to introduce myself. When I reached for Helen's hand, she smiled, and I saw at once that she was missing her upper two front teeth; there was just an empty gap where they should be, like a six-year-old might have.

That day at lunch, I heard a little of Helen's story. She had a slight lisp without her teeth, and so it was difficult to get her talking. She drank alone, she said. Mostly at night, at home, starting in the late afternoon after she was done at her job at an insurance company.

I nodded my head. "I drank alone a lot, too," I said.

"Sometimes," she continued, "it took a while to find my bottle and I'd start to tear the house apart looking."

"But wait," I mumbled through a mouthful of sandwich. "I thought you said you lived alone."

"I do!" she answered. "I hide the bottles from *myself*. I get drunk at night and then, oh, I get a little sad and cry. I decide I don't ever want to drink again. Then the next day, I change my mind and I have to find the bottles."

I hoped it was okay to laugh, because everyone at the table did.

Finally, she got to the part we were all wondering about. "I guess I walked into a wall or something," she said, gesturing toward her mouth. "I knocked out my front teeth. That's part of what got me here. I came on my own."

A lot about Helen's story rang a bell. I, too, came on my own. And hadn't Dave said I'd been falling down a lot? That could have been me with missing teeth! And who knew more about hiding bottles than I did? Plus, Helen had a house, a car, a job.

I decided I had more in common with Helen than with any of the other residents.

ऽ

Among the small group of patients I'd become friends with, Geneva was the first to go home. People "commenced" at a small afternoon ceremony in the great room on Fridays. The counselors would say a few kind words and give the resident a certificate of completion. Then it was the patient's turn to say something.

Geneva's longtime partner, June, a sturdy, athletic-looking woman with abundant freckles, showed up for the event. When it was time for Geneva to say a few words, her tough exterior gave way. She spoke quietly and vulnerably about how she had made meth into her lover. Now she was terrified that if she didn't quit, she'd lose June, the *real* love of her life, her best friend in the world.

As Geneva spoke, recognition slowly dawned on me. The way she described her feelings for June and meth were exactly how I would describe my feelings about Dave and drinking. I had lived in terror of losing him, yet I'd made alcohol my first love. I had much more in common with Geneva than I'd thought.

I happened to be sitting next to Nicole, one of the young moms

58

I'd gotten to know a little. She was pretty in a strange way—dark, curly hair that she wore in one large ponytail atop her head, which made me think of ballerinas.

Nicole had lost custody of her three children when it was discovered that she'd been driving her kindergartner to school while drinking. "The cops usually don't check the sippy cup," she'd explained to me one morning over a breakfast of rubbery eggs and expired yogurt.

At the time, my reaction had been suppressed horror. How could she do it? And using a sippy cup!

Now, I glanced over at Nicole's hands, clasped tightly in her lap. I noticed that her nails were bitten down to raw nubs. I felt a small, unexpected wave of compassion. Maybe Nicole was doing the very best she could as a mom. What if, in her own way, she loved her children just as much as I loved mine?

As I pondered this, a long-forgotten fact, a buried memory, rose to my mind. Suddenly I knew that this was the *real* reason Nicole's drunk driving with her kids in the car had struck such an chord of judgment in me. I had done the very same thing back in Oregon when my own kids were still young.

It happened sometime after I'd married Dave. No doubt more than once. But my memory was of a time when I was driving my boys to meet my ex-husband over a snowy mountain pass. Convinced that a drink or two would help me cope with the boring two-hour drive, I'd sipped wine coolers from a Diet Coke can, all the while telling myself I was perfectly fine to drive.

How could I have forgotten that?

Reluctantly, I recalled something else. How during that same era I had dutifully contributed to MADD (Mothers Against Drunk Drivers). I must have thought that a mom who contributes to MADD couldn't possibly be a drunk driver herself. But I was. And some part of me knew it. Why else had I memorized the ABCs backwards, except that I had heard a rumor it was one of the so-briety field tests police might give you?

Now, I could just imagine how my speech might have gone had I ever got caught: "But occifer, I'm a mom," I'd slur. "I'm a Chrishun! I belong to MADD!"

⚘

After we all hugged Geneva good-bye, I joined Nicole on the back patio. She glanced sideways at me, her blue eyes dark within the depths of her sweatshirt hood, which she wore often. "Do you think she'll make it?" she asked, meaning Geneva.

"I don't know. Supposedly, only one and a half of us will," I said, referring to the grim recidivism rate we'd heard about.

Nicole nodded. Took a drag on her cigarette. "How about you be the one person and I get to be at least the half?" She laughed, but it rang hollow.

"I drove my kids drunk, too," I blurted. "Over a mountain pass in winter."

"Yeah," she said, unimpressed. "Didn't we all?"

Didn't we all? I knew Nicole didn't mean that we'd all done that particular thing, but didn't we all do something equally inexcus-able?

By now, a few other residents had joined us outside. I was aware of their chatter, but my mind was somewhere else. Summing up my time here so far, I suppose. I was trying to convince myself I'd come a long way. I had worked hard to connect with other people and to focus on our similarities instead of our differences.

But if I had come far, it was only because I had so far to come. If I were going to be honest with myself, which for some reason I was determined to do, then I had to admit that Geneva'd been right. I *had* thought I was better than my fellow residents. In fact, hadn't even my benevolent efforts to find commonality been tinged with condescension? As if it was big of me to try to be one of them?

I played with the tab on my Coke, snapping it, thinking. I wasn't an awful person. But I had gotten so much wrong. The truth about who I was in relation to every person here could not be measured in degrees, by the sum of our similarities, or by adjusting for differences in lifestyle, sexual orientation, or socioeconomic factors.

I wasn't more like Helen, or less like Geneva. I was exactly like every single one of them.

ᔕ

It seemed like my worst nightmare had only just come true when, too soon, it was almost over.

One of our final activities was an afternoon spiritual retreat with a local pastor who was also on staff at the center. Normally, these retreats took place at a park up in the mountains, but since a freak spring blizzard had hit the area, we held ours at the pastor's church.

I hoped for something majestic, the kind of building where you sense God's power and grandeur. Instead, it was small and crummy and it smelled like a nursing home. But I liked the pastor. He asked us to find a quiet place anywhere in the empty building and write a letter to ourselves about our powerlessness over alcohol.

After wandering around the dim, narrow hallways, I came upon some combination of a nursery and toddler room. There were cribs, but there were also toys lying all over the blue shag carpet.

I sat in a rocker and tried to ignore the faint scent of diaper pail. Glancing around, my eyes fell on a Fisher-Price barn. The one with the plastic, round-headed people and the door that moos when you open it. As soon as I saw it, I was hit by a strong, visceral memory of my raw enthusiasm for that barn when I was a child.

As I settled in to write, I realized I was still ambivalent about the assignment. I knew I needed help with my drinking problem. And my life *did* feel completely unmanageable, as I'd been living it. But something about saying I was powerless over alcohol didn't wash. Wasn't it defeatist to keep declaring yourself too weak to say no? How would admitting that you can't resist drinking help you to do so?

Adding to my doubts were some old tapes in my head from my past. "You can't just say you're powerless over sin," they reminded me. "What about Paul's advice to 'fight the good fight'? What about God's promise not to give us any temptation greater than we can handle? If a Christian is no longer a slave to sin, how can you claim to be powerless over alcohol?"

Ironically, these were the same verses I had often used to convince myself I *should* be able to quit drinking.

Finally, I started to write. At first, it felt strange to write to myself in the second person. I started by addressing my youngest self, the one who loved the Fisher-Price barn. Then I wrote about my father's descent into mental illness. My parents' divorce when I was seven. My deep sense of inadequacy through adolescence. My first failed marriage. My desperation for Dave's approval, and my slow descent into alcoholism.

Slowly, a pattern emerged of a girl who was always striving, working hard to feel safe, to fit in, to garner affection and praise, to achieve success, to win at a contest she couldn't even name. The less the world cooperated, the more determined she became to control events and people around her. And the more she failed, the more she drank and the worse she felt, until one day she couldn't go on.

Realizing I was crying, I tried to find a Kleenex to blow my nose and couldn't. So I used some baby wipes. Later, as my tears gradually subsided, my breath came in little lurches, like a toddler's after a huge tantrum. In that moment, I felt powerless. But I also felt a sense of well-being and calm similar to what I'd experienced that morning when I sobbed by my bed.

Maybe surrender has to happen more than once.

When the pastor rang a bell to call us back from various shadowy corners of the church, we all came straggling toward the small fellowship hall filled with saggy, plaid-upholstered couches. While we ate our sack lunches, I felt small in the universe and yet so large inside. I felt cleaned out, raw-edged, and reborn.

It was raining softly outside while inside the six of us talked about God, our fears, our insecurities and questions. As we all chatted in the fading afternoon light, a couple people confessed that they had not expected to experience anything of God, but to their surprise they had. Everyone had written something.

As I listened to people talk, a great many questions still lingered in my mind about how my life could have brought me here, and how I would reconcile recovery with my battered faith. I was still somewhat in shock. And baffled by it all. Yet I left that little church knowing I'd found something infinitely more important than answers. And that was hope.

PART TWO

• eight •

PROOF OF LIFE

I wandered through my house feeling strangely detached, like I was taking one of those historical tours of a cabin or a castle where a famous person once lived. *There's the corner desk where she tried to write a novel and failed. There's her closet—note the pile of clothes and shoes on the floor (she was widely rumored to be a slob). There's the leather couch where she sat and drank her wine while watching TV…*

Evidence of my former existence was everywhere. Nothing had changed since I'd left for Pueblo weeks ago. And yet, when I arrived home for good on a sunny Friday afternoon in late April, I barely recognized the place. For all practical purposes, I had gone missing from my own life.

I wasn't looking for the self who recently lived here—the crazy drunk lady. I was looking for some other, better self—the one who vanished years ago, abducted by alcohol. Somewhere in the back of my mind, I'd always assumed that once I got sober, she'd come racing back into my arms with wails of relief.

It didn't happen that way. Instead, I began to worry that she'd

67

been held captive by alcohol for so long that, like a kidnap victim with Stockholm syndrome, she'd become enamored of, even loyal to, her captor. What if she no longer knew who she was apart from alcohol? What if she'd finally been set free, only to decide she didn't want to be?

What if she was dead?

After opening and shutting the refrigerator door several times, finding nothing I wanted there, I lugged my suitcase upstairs to our bedroom, letting it tip over with a loud bang on the hardwood floor. One of the case's small plastic feet was broken and had been for years, prompting Dave to ask every time we took a trip, "How can you stand to use a wobbly case like that?"

I couldn't tell him that I didn't mind an unstable bag as long it had plenty of compartments in which to hide alcohol. Now I could finally buy a new case. It was an idea that should have brought relief, given how worried I always was that my bag would get searched and bottles would come spilling out of my underwear.

Instead, the thought of a new bag made me feel a little panicked.

Moving on to the bathroom, I paused to stare at my reflection in the mirror. The whites of my eyes looked as bright as newly bleached teeth. As I marveled at the difference, I also noticed the lower half of my mirror was covered with a fine splatter of toothpaste spit, probably more than a month old. The counter was cluttered and grimy, too. *No wonder Dave moved into the guest bath years ago.*

On impulse, I leaned over the sink to examine more closely one of the larger globs of spit. Surely, if I got this spit tested in a high-tech lab, it would contain miniscule traces of alcohol. Which meant that when I washed my mirror, I would be destroying evidence. But evidence of what? A crime? Or a love affair gone bad?

It wasn't the evidence I'd hoped to find. What I wanted was proof of life. I wanted evidence that I was still *real*, still here, still alive inside myself. I needed a reason to believe that I was coming home, not just physically but emotionally and spiritually, too.

ᔕ

The most amazing thing about being an alcoholic or addict who suddenly gets sober is that from now on the time line of your life will always have a thick black line separating before you quit from everything that comes next.

But when you're standing with your back up against that black line, you wonder how on earth you can possibly go forward. It feels like your life will either stay blank or contain nothing but lies, a story about you that can't possibly be true. How could it, when you can't get your mind around this bizarre idea that you will no longer drink?

Ever. For *forever*.

My mind flashed back to when my son Nathan used to be afraid of heaven. He would cry every night about it, how he didn't want to go there.

I couldn't understand it. Why would someone not want to go to heaven? No matter how much I made it sound like Disneyland, I couldn't change his mind. Finally one night, when we were debating the issue yet again, I heard him. I understood that he wasn't afraid of heaven, he was afraid of living forever.

"Forever! And forever!" he wailed. "I don't want to live forever."

I got it now. Nothing seems like it should last forever, least of all a commitment to sobriety.

Later, as I unpacked the broken bag with all the handy compartments, I comforted myself with the knowledge that *someday*, chances were, probably, hopefully, I would get to drink again. Like maybe when I got very, very old. No one cares if a ninety-year-old drinks, do they?

Or what if a terrible tragedy occurred? What if I got into an accident or contracted a terminal illness? Surely, no one could begrudge me a drink then.

Or what if Dave died? Since he's fifteen years older, chances are...*But wait. I don't want Dave to die. Not even so I can drink. So what if it was just my dog that died?*

I debated this, as if Edmund's demise might be imminent. A pending option. By my calculations, it would have been worth at least a weeklong relapse.

ß

People were naturally curious. "How does it feel to be sober? How are you *doing*?"

I couldn't bear to tell them that I was secretly plotting my dog's death. I also couldn't make up my mind how I felt about being sober.

I adored being sober.

And I hated it, too.

In almost equal measures.

Sometimes in the course of a single hour.

Spring is a lovely season for being awakened from a twelve years slumber in the bottom of a bottle. Mornings, I woke up feeling like Sleeping Beauty—as though God had kissed me awake from a bad dream. I was so happy to feel good and clean and healthy, and remember the previous evening, that I wanted to skip down the sidewalk in front of our house.

Afternoons were predictably different. Do you have any idea how long a day can last when you're an alcoholic and there's no drink to look forward to at the end of it?

By two or three o'clock, the bubbly amazement I felt in the morning had gone flat. From four to six, time thickened and slowed. The minutes took on a horrible droning quality, like the sound of a distant chain saw, or a dentist's drill you can hear from the waiting room.

The pain felt somehow once removed, but constant.

As expected, Dave's homecoming was the hardest part of my day. I'd greet him at the door with a forced smile, bright eyes, and alcohol-free breath. But inside, I felt strangely bereft. We'd stand around the kitchen drinking sparkling water, gazing shyly at one another. Finally, one of us would mumble something about how good this was, us being sober. And the other would agree.

The big difference was that Dave *meant* it, highlighting again the fact that he wasn't an alcoholic like me. It didn't seem fair. Now more than ever, some puny, perverse part of me wanted him to be in the same beached boat, if for no other reason than to share my despair as I gazed out over the flat, parched land of the rest of my life.

Good thing I wasn't melodramatic.

The real problem with getting sober is that you remember why you drank in the first place. And the reason you drank in the first place was to *not* be sober. And the reason you didn't want to be sober was so that you didn't have to live in the real world with no means to muffle, enhance, or escape it.

At times, it felt like a mean trick.

But what was so bad about ordinary existence?

I couldn't understand it. I mean, I had a perfectly good life. So many obvious blessings. Why did I find it so difficult to live inside of a regular day in which nothing of great significance happened? What was it about simply being a human being stuck inside my body without a means of altering reality that I couldn't abide? Why was I so desperate to escape the natural state in which God made me?

And how come only humans have to suffer this way?

I thought about that a lot during those first long days at home alone with my dog. Often, I felt jealous of Edmund. It bugged me, the way he was so content to find a spot of sun on the floor and bask in it. The way he didn't need to find meaning in any day beyond where he left his bone the night before. The way he was grateful for the smallest things—a walk, a belly rub, a dropped piece of cheese or bologna rind.

The way he didn't crave wine.

ى

In addition to such existential concerns, I was coping with the more practical aspects of not drinking. It's amazing how much work can go into *not* doing something.

Now, even those activities I used to enjoy—going out to dinner with Dave, for example—had lost their appeal. Who wants to pay big bucks for a fine Italian meal when you can't drink red wine with it? Likewise, unpleasant tasks and chores that once seemed only slightly tedious when accompanied by a drink, or at least the promised reward of one, now struck me as unbearable.

In the meantime, Dave and I struggled to find new and fun things to do that didn't involve alcohol, didn't formerly involve alcohol, or that wouldn't make me *wish* they involved alcohol.

We succeeded to a modest degree when we took up biking. This was something I'd never done while drinking, and nothing about it suggested I should, or even could, be drinking while doing it. (Although, now that I think about it, I could have put alcohol in one of those camel-style backpacks that you drink from through a tube...)

Dave and I had both owned bikes back in Oregon, but we rarely rode them. My memory is that I hated the idea of people around town seeing me on a bike. I felt exposed. Silly. The helmets were an assault to my dignity, and God knows I didn't have much to spare.

Now, I no longer cared how I looked to absolute strangers. Almost every night that first spring of my recovery, Dave and I would eat a quick dinner and then don our pointy, alien-looking helmets. Then we'd be off, trekking all over our new town, exploring unfamiliar streets and neighborhoods. On the way home, we'd stop for ice cream, arriving back at the house sweaty, tired, and glad to be alive.

For a few minutes, anyway. Speaking for myself.

A bright spot in early sobriety was that as awkward as it sometimes felt to be sober with Dave, at other times it felt like we got to fall in love all over again.

Gradually, I got over the shock of sober sex. I learned how to enjoy the intimacy of being fully present in bed. I liked being more intentional and able to measure Dave's responses and adjust accordingly. Slowly, sex became a way to express my affection instead of something that happened to me when I was drunk.

Still, I secretly worried that I was a snore in the sack when sober. Finally one night, we were driving home after seeing a foreign movie when I got up the nerve to ask Dave, "So, tell me. How was sex different when I was still drinking?"

When he didn't say anything for a while, my heart thumped. We stopped at a red light and I waited. I knew that he was trying to figure out how to break it to me gently.

When he finally spoke, his answer broke my heart. Only not in the way I expected.

"It was lonely," he said. "You weren't really there."

It hit me then for the first time that while drinking had helped me to escape many negative aspects of reality, I'd missed so many of the good parts, too.

ॐ

Meanwhile, Dave's obvious, enormous relief about my being in recovery filled me with guilt. How bad must things have gotten to make my husband so excited, so grateful for the simple fact that his wife didn't get blitzed today?

But as proud as he was of me, I think he was scared, too. And so was I. We both sensed that my sobriety was fragile, even precarious. Dave must have felt at times like he was holding a newborn baby while standing in a raft barreling through white-water rapids.

Neither of us was ready yet to revisit the past or talk about the black tunnel that we'd been crawling through for years, the tunnel that had finally led to a small hole of sky above, which in turn had finally led to this sweet air and sunshine we now breathed.

Every day, our relief was palpable. So real that you could rock it in your arms. But how long could it last? Every day I felt like I was being forced to walk along the very edge of that hole we'd so recently crawled out of. I felt like I was always on the verge of falling back in, waving my arms for balance.

How could I possibly do this for the rest of my life?

nine

PINE-SOL, SWEAT, AND FEARS

You would think that given the long, empty days I'd be anxious to start working again. But you'd be wrong.

During the final years of my drinking, I'd been turning freelance work away, afraid of my diminishing capacities as a writer and an editor. I couldn't tell Dave the real reason why, a few years prior, I had decided to work at home on my first novel. This way, no one could keep track of what I did or didn't accomplish on any given day. Plus, everyone knows that your first novel usually fails.

In the past, especially early in my writing career, I had always written nonfiction, much of it personal. But after I married Dave and my drinking took over, I had stopped writing out of my life. If I couldn't tell the truth, I had nothing to say. So I worked on other people's projects or wrote about things that didn't involve my talking about myself.

Eventually, just before we moved, I finished the novel and I even found an agent who loved it. But she couldn't sell it. I think the story was promising, the prose passable, but on closer inspection, it felt jumbled, almost as if the writer was hungover or not quite at capacity. Imagine that.

By the time we moved to the Springs, it was clear that my career as a novelist was dead in the water.

Now that I was sober, I should have started taking projects again. But the idea of going back to the same kind of work I'd been doing the whole time I was drinking made me want to get very drunk. I still had too much guilt and shame around working on other people's projects while I had been living a double life.

Plus, I was haunted by something I'd heard in treatment: "Once you're a pickle, you can't ever be a cucumber again."

At first, I had laughed this off as a joke. But on further reflection, it wasn't funny. Were they talking about our *brains*? Had I done permanent damage? I kept picturing one of my mother's old Kerr canning jars with my pale, pink brain floating inside of it, shriveled up, soft, and stupid.

During my final meeting with the staff psychiatrist, I finally got brave enough to ask him, "Will I ever feel smart again?"

He assured me that I would—eventually. Aside from some extreme cases he referred to as "wet brains," he said that an alcoholic's mind will heal itself, given time.

"How *much* time?" I was trying not to hold my breath.

"Depends," he said, glancing down at my chart. Then, "Give it a year."

"Will it heal all the way?" I asked. "So it will be a cucumber again?"

He gave me a funny look. "A what?"

"Oh, forget it," I said. "You know, the pickle thing." Suddenly I couldn't remember how it went, which felt like further confirmation that I was still a dill.

Now, what the doctor said would come in handy when I explained to Dave why I wasn't ready to work. As I planned my pitch, I felt like a little girl faking sick so she could stay home from school. I did that a lot growing up. I'd stick my forehead close to the red-hot coils of a wall heater in our bathroom.

Then I'd go complain to my mother. She'd always put her cool hand on my forehead and declare, "You're burning up!"

"Am I?" I'd ask sweetly.

Tired of the pickle metaphor, I put it to Dave straight. "I need to talk to you about work," I said. "I know I haven't brought home any money for so long, and I know it's not fair."

I think he was chopping something on the cutting board at the time. Looking the slightest bit exasperated about my timing, he stopped what he was doing and put down the knife so he could give me his attention.

I explained that I felt embarrassed and useless. Ashamed of not working. But I was afraid of working, too.

"Afraid of what?"

"I guess I'm afraid of the pressure," I admitted. "And of failing." I hadn't fully known this—how terrified I was of trying and failing—until it came out of my mouth.

"It's not that I don't want to work at all," I added, thinking, *Yes, that's it exactly!* "I mean, I guess I'm willing to help on a few projects here or there." *But please don't ask me to!* "But the doctor at treatment? He said it could take a year for my brain to recover."

"That long?"

I nodded, suppressing an urge to put his hand to my forehead.

It wasn't that I didn't think Dave would be understanding. I was worried that he'd want to take me up on the "projects here or there" part. But instead, he brushed my bangs out of my eyes and said, "Honey, we're okay. The money is not what matters. I want you to stay focused on being sober and healthy. Let's just agree that you're taking a year off."

I tried not to light up too much. "Okay," I said, my voice going serious. "A year. I'll take one year off." And then, in a stroke of what seemed like genius because it showed how seriously I planned to take this whole recovery thing, I added, "And I want you to know that I'll start going to those recovery meetings every day."

He nodded and went back to chopping. "Good for you," he said.

It was a done deal. A whole year's guilt-free vacation! Woo hoo!

But then, something began to niggle at me. It was the phrase "whole year." When applied to time off, it sounded like music to my ears. But applied to sobriety? A whole *year* without a drink? At this point, every *day* I didn't drink seemed like a miracle.

And why did I volunteer the thing about going to recovery meetings *every day*?

Surely Dave understood that it was just a figure of speech.

🌀

Back at treatment, I had exchanged phone numbers with Nicole of the sippy cup. We'd promised to stay in touch, to be friends on the outside.

But now, I hesitated to call her. Hadn't I gotten sober so that I could hang out with *regular* people without embarrassing myself and Dave? Nicole was twenty years younger than me, had never finished high school, had an estranged husband, and an open file with Children and Family Services. Plus, her ballerina looks belied the fact that she wasn't just an alcoholic. By now I'd learned that she was a meth addict and a prescription-pill popper, too.

It's one thing to form bonds with strangers amid the forced intimacy of treatment. But did I want to go shopping with Nicole? Did I want to invite her over for dinner?

I thought I might. Ever since I got home, I'd been realizing something that should have been obvious sooner. I had no friends to speak of.

Having moved to a new state only six months prior was part of the problem. But even back in our small Oregon town where I had lived for twelve years, I'd had very few friends and none who knew the truth about me.

In fact, I'd worked hard at *not* having friends, because they got in the way of my drinking. Friends ask you to do things that don't necessarily involve or center on alcohol. Plus, friends *expect* things, like birthday cards. Phone calls. For you to *care*.

I couldn't be bothered.

But now a deep loneliness was slowly breaking me open to the possibility that I might want a friend.

ⓢ

I began to explore various meetings around town. Up north, I discovered you got a more professional crowd. The room smelled of hand lotion and chewing gum. Some of the men wore ties, and I noticed several women with manicures. You could almost imagine that you were at a business meeting instead of a gathering of drunks.

The meetings closest to my house, however, were held in an old, grungy building downtown. The room had a stained blue carpet and a bullet hole in the door window. The ceiling was way too low, the light depressingly dim, and the air smelled faintly of burned coffee, used vacuum bag, and human desperation.

Here you had all kinds. Street people, grandma types, the young and pierced, businessmen in suits, teachers, lawyers, and stay-at-home moms. There was even a small just-out-of-jail contingent and a self-professed purse snatcher. I had never in my life seen such a strange array of humanity gathered together in one place.

I could have chosen a less diverse meeting to make my "home group" (the one you attend regularly). But something about this motley crowd appealed to me. You got the sense here that everyone in the room was in dire need of, on the verge of, or in the middle of a miracle.

In the coming weeks, almost every day at noon I came to this room. I'd arrive just in time to get weak coffee with dry creamer in a Styrofoam cup and find a chair in the back against the wall. I'd sip my coffee, hug myself protectively with one arm, and wait for the introductions to come around to me.

"I'm Heather and I'm an alcoholic," I'd say, trying to let it sink in.

After some introductory readings, the gentle thrum of voices would begin, one picking up where another left off. Something about the steady murmur, like waves gently lapping on a rock, calmed me. Slowly, the shock of finding myself here—stripped of all my usual ways of labeling and identifying myself as something other than a recovering drunk—would fade away.

I noticed with relief that, unlike at treatment, many people here described their drinking histories in ways that echoed mine. I wasn't the only one who hid her drinking from a spouse. Or who blacked out a lot. Or who lied on a regular basis. I wasn't even the only Christian in the room who was surprised to find herself unable to escape her addiction through repentance and prayer.

I was not so special or unique after all. My surprise seems naïve to me now, but at the time, it was genuine.

As I got into the rhythm of daily meetings, I began to understand why newcomers are so strongly encouraged to attend ninety meetings in their first ninety days. Every time I walked into the room, at least several people said hello to me by name. They seemed glad, even relieved, to see me. They invited me to coffee afterward, an invitation I routinely declined.

Before I rushed off, invariably someone would call out, "Keep coming back! You're in the right place."

I heard that so often that I began to think it might be true.

※

One day, I sat down in a meeting next to a red-bearded man in a cowboy hat. As soon as the meeting opened for discussion, he introduced himself as Danny, choked up, and began to sob. I listened with growing horror as he explained that the night before his fifteen-year-old son had committed suicide.

"I didn't know what to do, so I came here," Danny said, swiping at tears.

Even as my heart broke for this man's loss, I couldn't believe my ears. *His son died just last night and so he came to a recovery meeting today?!* Didn't he have a family? A church? A therapist? A best friend? It just seemed so odd to me that he should be sitting here so soon after such an unimaginable tragedy.

I tried but couldn't imagine what I would do if Noah killed himself or overdosed. Ever since I got sober, without alcohol to numb my emotions and blur my thinking, I feared more than ever for Noah's life.

The couple times I'd talked to him since I got out of treatment, I could tell he was wasted. I could tell he had to harken way, way back in his memory to recall me: *Oh yeah, it's that woman again. The one who buys me underwear for Christmas and is always asking how I am and is always bugging me to call more often. Why did I answer?*

I knew Noah was genuinely glad for me that I'd gotten sober. But I also got the distinct impression that my recovery felt threatening, too. Which I totally understood.

Once, back when I worked for a Christian publisher, I attended a work retreat where author Brennan Manning was the speaker. Even though I loved his books, I spent the entire weekend avoiding him. I knew he was an alcoholic in recovery and I worried that the statement "It takes one to know one" might prove true. What if Manning took one look at me and saw the secret alcoholic hiding behind the Christian costume?

Plus, I didn't want to catch what this guy had.

Now, it was Noah's turn to keep his distance.

ꕤ

As Danny quietly wept and the meeting continued around me, I listened as people spoke gently about how they themselves had handled calamity and loss without having to drink. Some people wept discreetly. Others touched Danny's back as they walked past him to get coffee. The love and compassion in the room was palpable. And I finally got it: *Danny is here because this* is *his family.*

After that, I quickly figured out that these folks didn't know each other only because they hung out for an hour at lunch. They had formed a tight-knit community that happened largely outside of this room. They helped one another move, or went bowling or played poker together. They hosted each other on holidays and celebrated sobriety milestones as "birthdays."

You'd think a close-knit community like this would feel at least vaguely familiar to me, that it might be reminiscent of church in some way, or of small groups I'd been part of. But the particular brand of love and loyalty that seemed to flow so easily here wasn't like anything I'd ever experienced, inside or outside of church.

But how could this be? How could a bunch of addicts and alcoholics manage to succeed at creating the kind of intimate fellowship so many of my Christian groups had tried to achieve and failed?

Many months would pass before I understood that people bond more deeply over shared brokenness than they do over shared beliefs.

ॐ

On a muggy Saturday in June, everyone at the noon meeting was encouraged to come back later to help clean all the white plastic chairs we sat in. The chairs were getting grimy, and no one could recall when they'd last been washed.

I had nothing better to do, so I went. About a dozen other people showed up, too, which surprised me a little. I had assumed that since they weren't offering food as an incentive, few people would come. I didn't yet understand how strongly these people prized service to others as a means of staying sober.

As soon as I walked in the door, I regretted coming. I felt shy and out of place.

But before I could leave, someone handed me a large roll of paper towels. So I grabbed a chair and got on my knees and started to clean. A potbellied man with a hangdog face who reeked of cigarettes settled next to me. His name was Al, and we shared a bottle of Pine-Sol.

While Al and I worked quietly, I listened to the easy banter and occasional laughter of women around me. A small lump of longing formed in my throat. Would I ever feel like I could join in? Would I ever get a chance to prove that I had a great sense of humor, too?

I knew these people welcomed me, but I still didn't feel *part of* the group.

Which was my own fault. I showed up late to meetings and fled as soon as they ended. I couldn't bear the anxiety of hanging around to mingle and chat. What if no one spoke to me? What if I was left standing there, looking stupid?

It didn't occur to me yet that I might not be the only person who felt shy, or that I was just as capable of starting a conversation as anyone else. As had been my habit all of my life, I hung back and waited to be pursued by someone who was more willing to take risks than I was.

By the time we finished cleaning all the chairs that Saturday, it was raining outside. The kind of warm, harmless rain you get in early summer. As I hurried down the street to where I'd parked, my feet slapping on wet pavement, I heard other people laughing and squealing as they dashed to their cars.

On the drive home, my windshield wipers squeaking, I noticed that my hands smelled like disinfectant, and that I had managed to work up a light sweat. But as I neared my house, all I could think of was how I wished there were more chairs to clean.

§

What I can see now that I couldn't see then was that up until I got into recovery, my lifelong fear of people had effectively kept at bay any longing I might have had to be part of an actual community. Even at church, I had always been more interested in performing than in participating.

But now, a new and unfamiliar desire for connection rose up in me. It was like waking up hungry for a strange kind of food you've eaten only in dreams. I could almost taste what it would feel like to belong.

As much as I still dreaded the idea of picking up the phone, I began to understand that if I wanted to stay sober, I needed to reach out. If I wanted to learn how to live again, I needed to learn how to love people.

And if I wanted to give and receive the kind of raw intimacy I'd experienced in treatment, I should call Nicole. Finally, I did. As we began to hang out together, I discovered there was much more to her than I'd learned over rubbery eggs in treatment. Slowly, I got to know the desperately shy Nicole who flamed red whenever she got called on in a meeting. I got to know the Nicole who secretly nursed an eating disorder. I got to know the Nicole who loved her kids—and yet seemed so much like a kid herself that I wanted to take her home and feed her warm oatmeal.

In retrospect, I should have seen Nicole coming. And I should have seen her going, too. I should have known she'd break my heart.

But I didn't. For now, I was grateful to have Nicole to sit next to at meetings. She was someone to whisper with about the old, creepy men who were too interested in hugs. She was someone I thought that I could help to stay sober, which might help me stay sober, too. I heard it was supposed to work like that.

Eventually, I was slower to race off after meetings, and I got to know other people, too. Random, kind people who looked nothing like me on the outside but who turned out to be a lot like me on the inside.

One day, a woman named Lisa introduced herself. After a meeting, she took me to a drive-through coffee stand and then drove us all over town with no real destination, frantically smoking, windows rolled down, talking about everything from God to sex to children. She turned out to be an editor, too. She was fierce and frank and funny.

Suddenly, I was someone with two friends.

I felt like I had grasped the first couple rings of a construction paper chain like kids make in elementary school. I sensed that a string of such connections would eventually put me in the middle of something like a community.

But everyone knows how easily those paper chains can rip and break.

• ten •

THE BIG EMPTY

The trouble began when some old friends from Oregon swung through town and asked Dave and me to join them for dinner. Over the years, we'd shared many lovely meals with this couple. On almost every occasion, they drank wine in a perfectly sociable, acceptable way. Neither they nor Dave had any idea that every time I took my purse to their powder room I was doubling or tripling what I drank at their table.

But now, just the thought of seeing them made my mouth water. And not for water.

Where was Susan with her tea when I needed her?

Because I knew our guests would be drinking wine with dinner, and they'd be surprised when we didn't, I was anxious to manage a potentially awkward situation. I encouraged Dave to go ahead and have a little wine with them.

The restaurant where we met was the kind of fancy place that serves red and white wine in different-shaped goblets; the kind that suggests which wine to pair with each course; the kind that when you drink copious amounts of alcohol, you're made to feel cultured rather than like a lush. In other words, the kind of restaurant I used to *love*.

For the first half hour, things went fairly well. We ordered appetizers, I sipped sparkling water, and our friends ordered a bottle of wine for the table. When the salad course arrived and everyone (except for me) agreed that the red wine tasted "like rose petals," I began to sweat a little. *Rose petals!* I'd always preferred Chardonnays, but a good, deep red...

Sometime after the entrees arrived, I watched greedily as a server refilled Dave's glass before it was empty. It reminded me how upset I used to get if a server poured even a half-inch more wine in Dave's glass than mine. *Don't you see what you're doing, you stupid wench?* I wanted to scream.

Before I knew it, I began to vicariously taste every sip of wine Dave took.

Even as I pretended to enjoy the conversation, even as we asked after our friends' kids and they after ours, all I could think about was the empty ache of craving deep in my chest. By the time dessert—accompanied by port for everyone but me—arrived, I was seething with self-pity, which I hid with aplomb until we'd hugged our friends good-bye.

On the way home in the car, I confessed to Dave, "That was the longest dinner I've ever endured in my entire life."

"I thought you did so well," he said.

"Which part went well?" I asked. "The part where I was sipping water with my pesto gnocchi? The part where I had to listen to everyone else talk about red wine like rose petals? The part where everyone—including *you*—was enjoying port with dessert? Which part went well?!"

"Wow. I had no idea," he said.

"Why would you?" I answered snidely. "*You* were having fun!" For the rest of the twenty-minute ride home, I worked hard to pick a fight with Dave. Didn't he realize that he was supposed to barely sip the wine, not actually enjoy it? Didn't he know how hard this was for me? Didn't he think it was wrong to take total advantage of the situation? To have port!?

At first Dave tried to defend himself. Then he tried to apologize. Eventually he just fell silent. Clearly, I wasn't in a listening mood.

As soon as we walked in the house, I stomped directly to the laundry closet where, on a high shelf, we still kept an oversized bottle of red wine. I had insisted that we should have it on hand, just in case unexpected company dropped by. I wanted everyone to understand that it didn't matter to me *at all* if they drank in front of me.

Oblivious to the irony, I got on my tiptoes and grabbed the Merlot. In the kitchen, I banged open the utilities drawer and loudly fished out the bottle opener, hoping Dave would hear me and guess what he had caused. I didn't grab a wineglass, however, since that would have diluted the high drama I had in mind. The plan was to slug straight from the bottle.

I charged upstairs to my den and slammed the door. Sitting on my small couch, hugging the wine to my chest, I finally let myself cry—loudly enough, I hoped, for Dave to hear. I stared at the beautiful label on the bottle. I stroked the dark glass. As time passed, and Dave failed to come knocking on the door so that I could scream at him to get out, I wept even harder.

Then, in a sudden moment of clarity, I saw myself sitting in a dark room, snot-faced and rocking a large bottle of Merlot like it was my baby—and I broke out laughing. I was still angry and hurt, but I began to see the humor in the whole thing, too. Including how ridiculous it was to expect Dave to drink without drinking.

I went downstairs and put the bottle away. When I climbed into bed beside Dave, he was already gently snoring. It hit me then that we'd survived our first fight since I got sober. I wanted to wake him up and say, *Honey! Do you realize this was the first real argument we've had since I got sober!? Isn't that amazing?!*

The next morning, I apologized. Even though Dave had no idea how close I came to drinking, I felt like a fool in front of myself. Who knew I could still go crazy at the drop of a cork?

۵

A week after the wine-like-rose-petals fiasco, I was flipping through a Pottery Barn catalog when I came to a spread that featured beautiful wine carafes and glasses on an elegantly set table. The glasses were filled with what looked like a smooth, buttery Chardonnay. I tried to tell myself it was probably just yellow water or apple juice.

But what if it *was* real wine? Who got to drink it after the photo shoot?

I tried to turn the page, but my hand wouldn't move. Probably because it was still holding the glass in the photo, lifting it to my lips...

After I finally managed to shut the catalog, I decided to try a trick I'd been taught in treatment. "Think the drink through," one of the counselors had said. Think all the way through to what would happen if you took a drink.

So, what would happen? I asked myself.

I would feel relief. I would feel that soft, warm, soothing feeling flowing back through my veins. I would feel fulfilled and something close to whole again. I would feel held together, like I was one with my desire and was giving my deepest self what it craved.

But for how long?

For a while.

And then what?

I'd want more.

And then?

It would begin to fade, and I would want another drink, another glass.

And then?

Well, more!

But if what you crave is alcohol, then how come it never truly satisfies you?

It was a good question. Since I hadn't had a drink in a long time, I obviously wasn't experiencing physical craving, and I was way past the stage of withdrawal. So where did this deep sense of want and longing come from?

To my surprise, it was hard to articulate an answer. All I could say was that this mysterious, powerful thirst seemed to emanate from an empty place deep inside my soul that ached to contain or hold something I could not name—and its absence *hurt*.

I drank to numb that pain.

Now, I stood at the edge of an internal abyss that felt as deep and wide as the Grand Canyon. Unless I found a way to fill that empty space, how would I ever be able to stay sober?

Granted, I figured that my inner emptiness was spiritual in nature. No doubt beneath the surface of my craving for alcohol was a deeper longing for more of God. But I resisted this diagnosis. Not because I didn't believe on some level that it was true, but because I'd been there, done that.

ॐ

I always felt that I didn't find God so much as I stole Him from my sister.

When Katherine was about twelve and I was nine, she found Jesus. She caught and rode the tail end of the Jesus Movement of the late sixties and early seventies. She joined Jesus clubs, went to

Jesus camps, pasted Jesus stickers on her guitar case, and read Jesus books. Any appeal Jesus might have had for me was ruined by His misguided association with her.

One of my sister's favorite ways to explain my animosity was that I had a hole in my soul that was shaped like a cross. Everyone has this hole, she said. And you have to ask Jesus into your heart to fill it. The idea made a lot of sense to me. Even at a young age, I could feel the hole she was talking about.

But Katherine was the good girl, not me. I was the designated bully in the family. The mean one. I couldn't bear the idea of becoming a Christian Goody-Two-Shoes like her. Plus, I knew that my siblings would all laugh at me. What would they think if I tried to be nice?

I preferred my role as the one who would chase you with a butter knife or who would break down your bedroom door if you crossed me and tried to lock me out.

At the time, my mother and stepfather regularly attended the Presbyterian church in town and usually dragged us kids along. But this kind of churchgoing didn't count in Katherine's eyes. You had to be born again and wear that label. You had to ask Jesus into your heart and then worry a great deal about getting everyone else to do the same so they wouldn't go to hell.

My sister's campaign relied heavily on Christian tracts—little pamphlets with illustrated stories that depicted the perils of hell, the imminent coming of the Rapture, and the misery of life without Christ. She'd leave these tracts in my bedroom, on the back of the toilet, or casually lying around the house where she knew I'd find them.

Not all of the tracts were scary. But the one I remember most vividly featured a guy who dies unexpectedly in a car crash. Immediately he is standing before the Judgment Seat of Christ, where he is forced to watch a film (sans popcorn) of his entire life, emphasizing every horrible thing he ever thought or did.

The idea that God had a camera trained on me at every moment so that He could someday mortify me with my own bad behavior was so alarming to me that for a long time it lay waste to my sister's claim that God was pure Love. Easy for her to say, since her film could air on the Disney Channel.

It wasn't until I was around fifteen that I realized Jesus might be trying to woo me, too—right through the walls of my sister's bedroom. Some of the Christian music I heard coming from her stereo hurt my heart in a good way.

At some point, I began to sneak into her room when she wasn't home and read her Jesus books and listen to her Jesus albums and snatch little pieces of God. I was always careful to leave no trace that I'd been there or touched anything.

But clearly, something had touched me.

One night at the end of my sophomore year of high school, after a heartbreaking fiasco involving a boy, drinking, vomit, and an underage disco club, I crawled out of my bedroom window and sat on my roof. I stared out at the starry sky, feeling terribly sorry for myself. At some point, I sensed that Jesus was there next to me. Making His move on the mean sister.

Before I knew it, I was asking Jesus into my heart and whispering the prayer I knew you were supposed to pray. Given that I had attended Christian summer camps in the past and had emotional breakdowns on bonfire night, it probably wasn't my first attempt at conversion. But something about it—the cleanness I felt inside, the milky peace I floated in for weeks afterward—made it seem real this time.

After my rooftop conversion, I gradually came out to my family and friends. I joined a youth group and tried to spread my faith. I listened to all the Christian pop music my sister had tortured me with.

I married young, and for the next decade my first husband and

I tried to do what we thought good Christians should do. We latched on to a local church that seemed on fire for Jesus. We were careful to take notes on the sermon. We hung out only with other Christians who attended our church or a similar one. We listened only to Christian music and watched only wholesome TV.

For years, I carried my Bible everywhere, even to get my hair cut.

But then, somewhere along the way, things changed. I grew weary of what felt like the small confines of my faith. I became skeptical about a rigidly literal approach to the Bible. Increasingly, the list of rules I felt compelled to adhere to struck me as arbitrary. I resented being told how to vote and how to think. I sensed that we were focusing on all the wrong things.

In the meantime, I got the distinct impression from my fellow Christians that if you were a true believer, you weren't *supposed* to feel unfulfilled or empty, because that would mean that something was still missing from your life. And how could that be the case when you had Jesus? How could you still be thirsty when you had a river of life flowing out of your very soul?

Eventually, I sought fulfillment through other, predictable means. Success in my career. Being the parent of impressive children. Earning the adoration and love of a man. But no matter how many books I wrote, how many As my kids got, or how often I got the romantic attention I craved, it seemed like my heart was always emptying faster than I could fill it.

Even as I continued to go through the motions, my faith felt cumbersome and joyless.

What happened next is not what one would hope. Instead of recognizing that the local church I attended wasn't the only valid expression of Christianity on the planet, I stayed where I was and got cynical. Instead of asking new questions, I assumed that I was stuck with the answers I already had. I thought my only option was to put the lid back on my doubts and punch some airholes in the top.

I'm sure it's no coincidence it was around this time that my first marriage began to fall apart. As it became harder to breathe in church, it also became harder to find air in a marriage that had taken on the form and feeling of a sibling relationship. You know the rest of the story. Divorce, disillusionment, and drinking, all the while desperately clinging to what was left of my jaded Christian faith.

By the time I started dating Dave, I was secretly ready to trade the God I stole from my sister for a full refund. But I never paid anything for God in the first place, and everyone knows that God and all His gifts are supposed to be free.

So why did it feel like it cost so much?

eleven

NOT MY FATHER'S DAUGHTER

One sweltering day in July, I was sitting in an ordinary noon meeting next to Nicole, when I looked up and spotted my biological father.

There were about five of him in the room that day. Several of the men were involved with the nearby Salvation Army program. The other two had that rumpled, worn-out look that screamed *homeless*. None of these men were new to the meeting, or to me. But any one of them could have been my father.

The realization stunned me. How could I have been coming to this room for almost three months and missed this?

The answer was simple. Growing up, I always preferred to think of my dad as mentally ill with some drug issues rather than as an addict with mental issues. I knew that he abused his medications, but for some reason I preferred a version of the story that depicted him as a victim of wrongheaded doctors in the sixties who didn't know how to treat manic depression and got him hooked on amphetamines.

But now, sitting here in this room, old memories began to surface. Hadn't my father often lived in halfway houses for alcohol and drug addicts? And didn't he meet a woman he married and quickly divorced at a 12-step meeting for alcoholics? And didn't he leave behind dozens of empty beer cans that time when he abandoned his apartment?

The list went on. As the evidence mounted, I acknowledged in a way that I hadn't before that my father had been a drug addict and, quite possibly, an alcoholic, too.

But regardless of whether he was one or both, I was stunned by the sudden realization that he had sat in rooms exactly like this one. And it hadn't been enough to save him.

⑤

My parents divorced when I was seven. My father stayed on the East Coast, where I was born, and my mother returned to her hometown of Everett, Washington, with four kids, no money, and a lot of sadness. I wouldn't see my father again until I was thirteen.

Having been my father's pet, at least in my own mind, I took his sudden absence from my life very hard. From a distance, I idealized him. I imagined him to be the father I always dreamed of having, like the kind I saw on TV. I knew that he had called me his "impusbellyrupus"—"imp" for short. I coveted a single photo I had of him in which he wore a trench coat and looked to me a lot like Cary Grant.

In the meantime, when I was eight, my mother remarried. I hated my stepdad on sight, convinced that my mother should have waited for my "sick" daddy. Convinced, too, that she only married my stepdad because he bought her a four-slot toaster.

By the time I was twelve, my relationship with my stepfather had become so hostile and often violent that he gave my mother an ultimatum: *Get rid of Heather or I'll leave.* Since my mother wasn't amenable to raising four kids on her own, she sent me to live with my father.

That summer, he was living with twenty-three other people in a scummy, roach-infested brownstone in the Bronx. It was a half-way house for recovering addicts and alcoholics, but I don't think I quite understood what this meant, especially since I never saw my father or anyone else drink or use drugs.

Initially, I was thrilled to be reunited with my father. But after a couple days, I began to understand that he was too depressed to pay me much attention. He sat in his room alone and smoked, while I was left to watch soap operas all day with a blind African-American woman who expected me to narrate the action she couldn't hear: "He's hiding something in his coat pocket...She is glaring at him..."

If part of my mother's intention was to shock me into a new appreciation for what I had back home, it worked. The switch from my big green front yard, my ten-speed bike, and water fights with friends to a hardscrabble brownstone in an ugly part of the Bronx triggered remorse in me.

But my father saw an opportunity for redemption. He planned for me to stay permanently and wanted me to start school there in the fall. Which might have happened had he not made the mistake of allowing me to go visit a childhood friend in New Jersey.

Years ago, Kimmy's mom, Beverly, and my mom lived next door to each other and had been best friends. Beverly was appalled when she heard my stories about cockroaches frying in the pan with the chicken while the blind lady cooked our dinner. Or how I spent my allowance on food because there wasn't enough to go around. Or how I was terrified of the scary men on the corner who whistled when I passed by.

She was so taken in by my sweet side, which I reserved for strangers and teachers, that she couldn't understand how my stepfather could possibly have wanted to get rid of me, nor why my mother would let him. She got my mother on the phone and convinced her that she needed to let me come home.

I agreed to try to be good.

I returned to our house in Everett, Washington, in time for the school year. Things improved for a little while.

In the meantime, we got word that my father was "sick" again. I realize now that he must have had a relapse of some kind. He was booted from the house where I had stayed with him. And for a long time, I thought it was my fault. I don't remember who told me, but I learned that my father had been completely devastated by my decision to return home.

I remember sitting in math class back in Everett haunted by his sadness. I thought of him alone in that bedroom across from mine in the Bronx, raising and lowering his cigarette, a tiny orange spot moving in the dark. How I couldn't help him. How my being there wasn't enough. And how now my leaving was somehow the cause of a horrible crisis that had my mother and stepfather talking in hushed voices.

How could I have left him?

Some months later, we got a phone call from my father to let us know that he was hitchhiking his way across the country to come see us four kids. I was the only one of my siblings who had seen my father since the divorce. I felt like his coming was proof that I meant enough to him that he was willing to relocate in order to be near me.

Every few days, my father would call us collect from a state farther west to keep us abreast of his progress. My siblings were beside themselves with anticipation, ready to forgive him for not sending birthday cards with money inside, except to me.

But the closer to the West Coast my father got, the more afraid I began to feel. I couldn't explain why. Something in his voice wasn't right. Something was more wrong with him than whatever was wrong the summer I spent with him.

Somewhere around Wyoming, the police called to say that they'd arrested my father in a Dairy Queen. Apparently, he'd woken up that morning convinced that he was God, and when the people who'd been hankering for a peanut buster parfait that day wouldn't believe in him, he got angry, loud, and obnoxious.

They let him out of jail a day or two later. And within a week, he showed up on our doorstep in Everett. There he stood with a big silly grin and yellowed teeth and a lot of nervous twitches. He was wearing bowling shoes that he'd stolen from a bowling alley. But my mother and stepfather were kind to him and let him stay at our house the first night.

That night, after we'd all gone to bed, my father stayed up into the wee hours drinking coffee and smoking. Using an ink pen, he scrawled symbols, signs, and nonsensical notes in the enormous green atlas we kept on the coffee table in the living room.

In the morning, when he tried to explain to us what he'd written and why, it was clear that he was out of his mind.

Later that day, at my father's insistence, my stepdad drove him to nearby Seattle where he checked into a run-down old hotel.

A few days later, three of us siblings (my brother Andrew was deemed too young) went to visit him there. After climbing creaky, narrow stairs that smelled like old vomit, we found his door. Nailed to it was a handwritten note in my father's wild scrawl telling the devil to stay away.

After staring at the note for a while, we knocked on his door anyway, went in, and tried to be his kids. Tried to not be afraid. Tried not to smell the smells or look too close at the stained toilet and the bare, striped mattress on the metal cot. Whoever drove us there must have been waiting in a car somewhere.

After that, I think I remember a trip to a bowling alley, where my father let me win and laughed and cackled in a way that I loved. And maybe we went to the Space Needle, too. It's all vague, except for the part where he was suddenly back on our porch in Everett again, violently clapping his bowling shoes together to shake the dust of us off his feet in angry protest.

He was back to believing that he was God again, or something close to it. He announced he was flying back to New York. He didn't need money or a ticket. He could get on the plane if someone just dropped him at the airport.

Finally, my stepfather agreed and took him to Sea-Tac—thinking *good riddance*, I'm sure. And good luck with that. Even back then, when security was more lax, you couldn't just board a plane without a ticket, even if you happened to think you were God.

And yet, six hours later, my father called collect from New York. Safe and sound. "I walked right on," he said.

My mom and stepdad were stunned, disbelieving. But all I knew or cared about was that my father had come to see us, and we had made him mad. I thought of the people he'd frightened in Dairy Queen that day. And I remember thinking that we all should have just believed in him. Or at least pretended to.

What if I never saw him again?

᠙

I needn't have worried.

Throughout my teens and early twenties, my father was in and out of my life. At some point, his mental illness qualified him for disability. He lived mostly on the streets, in halfway houses, missions, and mental hospitals.

Frequently, my siblings and I received phone calls to let us know that—yet again—our father had tried to kill himself. *Real* hospitals were by far his favorite place to be, and to get in you can't just say you want to die; you have to *try* to die. So my father did whatever he had to do—drink rubbing alcohol or swallow razor blades—in order to get himself admitted.

Often, he experienced manic episodes that when left untreated escalated into paranoid psychotic behavior. It wasn't unusual for him to spend his disability money on taxis in order to run from nonexistent people he thought were chasing him.

Once, he called me breathless after a $350 cab ride to explain that they (vague but highly organized evil people) were definitely on to him. This was his final good-bye.

But not really.

After I was married, sometimes my father would come to visit us in Oregon. Tom and I would try to help him in various ways. To get him into an apartment, for example, or to find a way to get his disability check, since for obvious reasons the government had a hard time keeping a current address.

Always, after a week or two, something would go awry.

Once, he was arrested for stealing reading glasses from the Goodwill store. He needed them so that he could read the paper all day in a café while sipping his coffee slowly enough so that when the manager finally tried to kick him out, he could say in truth, "I'm still drinking my coffee."

After years on the streets, my father began to look like someone who lived there. Now and then, we'd be in some doctor's office or at a grocery store, and he'd embarrass me by going up to people and asking if they had a dime. Then, he'd look for someone he saw smoking and offer them a dime for a cigarette.

Now I wonder: Didn't I have a dime?

Or did my dad have a rule against taking his daughter's dime?

Or did I have a rule about not contributing to his smoking?

I cringe at the thought. It wouldn't surprise me to learn that

I begrudged my dad his cigarettes. I had all sorts of convictions and strident opinions in those days that were the opposite of what you'd think a person who professed to love Jesus would have.

§

One day, when I was twenty-three and still married to Tom, my dad called us from a jail in Arizona. He said he'd been put on a plane by a doctor at Oregon State Mental Hospital who used his disability money to buy him a one-way ticket to Arizona with nothing at the other end. When a hospital in Arizona wouldn't admit him, and it was 110 degrees outside, he'd gotten in a hospital van that was running by the curb "because it was air-conditioned." He was arrested a while later—but cooler, at least.

Could we bail him out?

No, we couldn't bail him out. We were young, dirt-poor, and had two kids. And besides, no one was going to fool us into thinking a doctor at the hospital actually took his money and bought him a one-way ticket to Arizona. Paranoia was the name of this game.

Then we got a phone call from a guy who worked at the hospital and also at a local halfway house in Salem, Oregon, where my dad often stayed. He was calling to tell us that what my dad said was true. This doctor really did this. We should do something about it. He'd be willing to testify.

I called the doctor. After a few minutes, he stopped denying it and started crying instead, begging me to not do anything, promising me that he would never do such a thing again. He mentioned his wife, his kid, and even—scout's honor—his *dog*.

Apparently, the hospital had temporarily lost its accreditation, which meant they weren't being reimbursed for my dad's care. My father was an awful nuisance. A drag on resources. Obviously, the doctor had no idea that someone out there cared what happened to him.

But did we care? That was what my dad wanted to know. If we cared we would sue. Please, you've gotta sue!

We saw a lawyer. He said he would take the case. But not without at least a thousand dollars for various fees along the way. The bummer, he explained, was that there was a cap when it came to suing the state. He didn't seem supermotivated, since it wasn't big money.

We didn't sue. Maybe I felt sorry for the doctor. Maybe he sounded like a nice man. Like a good father. Somebody's dad who at least came home every night to tuck his kid in. A dad who was present and accounted for, even if he did put people like my dad on airplanes. I can't believe now that I was so easily dissuaded—and, at the time, neither could my dad.

He was angry. He made it back to Oregon from Arizona a couple months later, and he went back to the same halfway house near the state hospital. One night he tried to take his life again, this time by way of an overdose of prescription pills.

As usual, he didn't leave a note. And as usual, his attempt appeared to fall shy of completion. He woke up the next morning and seemed fine. As was his habit, he went down the street to buy a paper. His housemates said he was upbeat at breakfast that morning, even a tad more optimistic than usual.

But then, while he was sitting with the paper and drinking his morning coffee, the drugs he'd taken, which had a significant built-in time delay, finally attacked his heart with a vengeance. I'm told that he turned red and began clutching at his chest. Panicked, he begged for an ambulance and for someone to save him. He didn't want to die, after all.

The call from the hospital came Memorial Day morning. Tom and I raced an hour up the freeway, but my father died before we arrived. The doctor let me go into the room where his body was lying on a table to say good-bye. It was the first time I'd ever seen a dead body, and I was taken aback by how obviously empty of a person it was.

I spent a good deal of my twenties coming to terms with his suicide and my guilt over it.

৯

After spotting my father in my meeting that day, I became keenly aware of all the men in recovery who reminded me of him. The ones who looked rumpled and defeated. The ones who tried to dress up, but their jacket was ill-fitting or their tie was stained. The ones who clung fast to their dignity because it was hanging by a thread.

For some reason, it troubled me greatly to think of my father as one of us. It pained me even more to think of him as someone like me, because it implied that I might be like him.

His story didn't exactly inspire hope. It didn't give me anything to hold on to. If recovery hadn't worked for my father, why should I believe recovery would work for me?

I frequently reminded myself, as I had all of my life, that I wasn't like him. My father didn't stick with recovery, but I planned to. And unlike me, my father had been arrogant, belligerent. A know-it-all. He was the kind of crazy that people saw right off.

I might be stubborn, I might be a drunk, but I wasn't my father's daughter.

twelve

HOLE IN THE WALL

One day after a meeting, Nicole and I walked by a little Israeli café. It had just barely opened. We looked in the window; there were no pictures on the walls, and the seats and tables looked cafeteria style and plain. Seeing no one inside, we felt sorry for the owners and agreed to give it a go.

"Soon enough all the drunks will find it," I assured Nicole.

She wondered aloud if they located it here on purpose, to be near all of us. "As long as they have coffee, they could have a crowd," she noted.

But they didn't have coffee. At least, not yet. So we ordered a hummus and pita bread plate to share, along with two Diet Cokes. Since we were the only table, I felt kind of bad about our puny order. But by now, I knew it was pointless to try to get Nicole to eat a real meal. As for me, I was saving room and calories for ice cream later. Sweets and desserts of all kinds were quickly becoming a new addiction.

We sat by the window and put the Styrofoam container between us. We talked while we ate, and after a while, we had so much hummus left over that I watched Nicole play with it for ten minutes, creating a volcano as high as it would go, then smashing it and starting again.

"I want to write a book," she said at one point. "I mean, I want you to help me write one. About my life."

This subject had come up before. I told her that would be great.

She said she was thinking that maybe when she had six months of continuous sobriety she would begin. "I'll just write all the stuff that happened to me and then you can take it and do stuff with it."

I laughed. "That could work," I told her. "But it has to sort of read like fiction. I mean, it has to have conflict, suspense, a story arc—"

"That's what you would do," she agreed. And then she smiled. "Add big words and stuff."

I laughed. "Yes, I could add big words."

"Like *animosity*," she pointed out.

"Yes," I said, laughing. I wondered if this was the only big word she thought she knew. But it fit. She had so much of it—*animosity*.

While Nicole straightened the frizzy bun atop her head, I suggested that six months might not be long enough for her to be sober before beginning a book. That she ought to have some things resolved first—or at least on their way to being resolved. I was referring to all her problems with her estranged husband and her DHS case, as well as the need for her to stay sober for more than a couple months at a stretch.

She nodded. "You're right." And she stuck her finger in the center of the hummus volcano a little harder than necessary.

And then I knew what she was thinking. *Fine, but not my dad. I won't forgive my dad.*

🌀

By now, Nicole and I had had a lot of conversations about God. Most of which spiraled back to her father, who raped her for the first time when she was twelve. Abandoned by both parents, Nicole grew up in foster homes—twenty, to be exact.

Nicole obviously believed in God. But she wasn't buying the God of the Bible. One afternoon, she told me about how her sponsor had asked her to list the qualities she wanted in a higher power. Nicole told her that she wanted God to love her. She wanted Him to help her. She wanted Him to forgive her. So far, so good, right?

But there was a glitch: She didn't want *her* God to forgive just anyone. The God of the Bible is *way* too easy, she insisted. Even a monster like her father could go to heaven if he repented. And, in her words, "Men who screw little girls shouldn't go to heaven."

How do you argue with that?

I asked Nicole once what she wanted to happen to her dad. What if vengeance could be hers?

She'd set him on fire, she said calmly. I could tell that she'd thought about this.

But could she? If her dad knocked on her door and offered to stand in the yard so that she wouldn't burn her carpet, and if he handed her the gasoline and a match and he even begged her to do it, could she?

I'm not sure she could. And if she couldn't, why should God have to?

In the meantime, I noticed that Nicole refused to pray along whenever someone closed a meeting with the Lord's Prayer instead of the Serenity Prayer. Standing there, holding her small, chapped hand with its bitten-raw fingernails, I heard the words through her perspective: *Our Father.*

How do you pray to "Our Father" when your own father is a monster who has never paid for his sins? Especially when you learn that if God had His way, He wouldn't make your father pay, either?

Who art in heaven. She wants her father to burn in hell. How does she pray to, much less imagine, a father in heaven?

Hallowed be thy name. His name is Dennis. And he's still out there somewhere, doing no one knows what.

Forgive us our trespasses, as we forgive others. Are you serious? She's supposed to forgive him?

Sometimes I would squeeze Nicole's hand a little as I prayed the words, remembering how late I came to love this prayer. I came to love it in my twenties only after a great deal of resistance for similar reasons. The father thing didn't work for me.

But through counseling and prayer and talking, I saw the problem clearly, and I didn't like it. Why should my father ruin my ideas about God? Still, I couldn't think of God as a father until after the day I had an experience in prayer where I let God hold me while I beat on his chest like a demon on Santa's lap.

But I knew Nicole wasn't ready to beat on God the Father's chest yet.

And if God tried to pick her up, he better first check her pockets for matches.

ॐ

Nicole and I had a lot in common. I didn't want to set my biological father on fire. It was too late for that, anyway—he'd been cremated. But there was a time when I would have gladly done my stepdad that favor, lit his socks on fire myself.

As I mentioned earlier, I was eight when my mother married my "bring me a beer" stepdad.

Even though Jon wooed us kids—bringing us gifts like Pop-Tarts, a sled, and chocolate milk—I resented him from the get-go. After he and my mother married, I hated him with a raw, cold fierceness that defied explanation. He gave me the shivers. He repulsed me. Now and then, he'd thump my head with his big thumb or he'd box my ears, or try to spank me.

As I got older, our conflicts escalated, often turning into violent brawls, since I always fought back. Once, after I'd had my appendix out, Jon threw me down a flight of stairs, reopening the surgical wound. I'm sure it hurt plenty, but what I remember most is feeling gratified. I didn't mind getting hurt if it made him look like a monster.

While these altercations unfolded in front of my mother, she usually cried and yelled and got hysterical. But she never tried to intervene. Later, she'd let me know that I was mostly to blame. "You egg him on!" she'd cry. "You egg him on, Heather!"

My mother was wrong to say this. And she was wrong to tolerate the kind of sporadic physical abuse I and my siblings occasionally suffered at my stepdad's hands.

But here's the rotten truth: *I did egg him on.* I knew exactly how, and to me the satisfaction was worth the risk.

When I was twelve, I decided that everyone hated me and I hated my stepfather and my whole life so much that it was time to die. So I went to my mother's medicine cabinet and chose the bottle of pills that had a label warning, "Do not exceed one pill in twenty-four hours." *Perfect.* I swallowed the whole bottle and then I lay down on my bed and waited to die.

And I waited. And I waited.

When nothing happened, I tried something else, too. I had heard that you could sniff hair spray to death. So I sprayed it a lot around the bathroom and tried to smell it and smell it until the can was empty. Then I lay down again on my bed and stared at the ceiling and waited to die. Again, nothing.

Sometime late that afternoon, while I was still on my bed and angrily waiting to die, my mother came home from work. A few minutes later she began to yell from her bathroom, "Who took all my hormone pills!?"

I don't know who was more pissed, me or my mother.

She called her doctor and told him what happened and he told her that I'd be fine, but I might start my period if I hadn't already.

For me, this was a possible bright spot. Maybe even something to live for. Today, I would become a woman!

But that didn't happen, either. The whole thing was a wash. And what I remember most now is how mortified my mother was. How *embarrassing* to have to tell her doctor that her daughter ate all her hormone pills.

ᔕ

To her credit, after I tried to kill myself, my mom took me to see a child psychiatrist—once. All I remember about our session is that the doctor smoked. I told him that this was a disgusting and stupid habit (my stepdad also smoked). I asked, "How could someone stupid enough to smoke expect to help anyone else?"

On the way home, my mother scolded me at great length, bemoaning again how much I embarrassed her. Later, she admitted to me that the doctor's only advice to her and my stepdad was to hang on somehow until I was eighteen.

But my stepdad couldn't hang on. Shortly after we saw "the shrink," as he referred to the doctor, he gave my mom the ultimatum that she sent me to the Bronx to live with my biological father. As you know from the previous chapter, that lasted for a summer.

After I was allowed to come back home, things improved for a little while. But nothing about the way I felt about my stepfather had changed. His presence made my skin crawl. The mysterious urge I felt to reach for a butcher knife never left me.

Soon, I would understand why.

I was thirteen when I made the discovery. I was lying on my bed one day after school when I thought I saw a small hole in the knotty pine wall of my bedroom. I got up to look closer and found a carefully drilled peephole in the center of one of the knots. It went through my bedroom wall into the basement workshop, where my brother and stepdad often fiddled with projects.

At first, I blamed my little brother for the hole. He vehemently denied it. Finally, my stepdad admitted that it was *his* hole. I don't remember how I got him to admit this. But it turned out that he'd been watching me through that hole since I was eight. Watching me dress for bed, watching me get into and out of our downstairs shower...

I don't recall my reaction on learning the news. Or my mother's. I blocked all that out. All I remember are the tidal waves of shame, scarlet red walls of utter humiliation that heated my body for weeks and months and years to come.

Now, I wonder why I felt so much shame for what he did.

I shared all of this with Nicole in the hope that I could help her. I wanted her to know that I understood that slimy, yucky feeling of having been violated. My stepdad had never touched my body, but I still grew up feeling raped.

But Nicole wasn't interested in my story. And she was right that it didn't compare to hers.

In the meantime, I had big dreams for her. I learned that she'd gotten her GED, and I thought she should go to college. I thought she should set about becoming someone more like me. More like who I wanted her to be. I thought she should find a way to forgive her dad. I thought she should learn to be a better mom. I thought she should let her kids hug her without asking permission.

Who did I think I was? And why didn't I see that I was working harder on Nicole's recovery than I was on my own?

thirteen

A SHINING EXAMPLE

Sometime in August, I got a phone call from my sister, Katherine, who was still living in the same central Oregon town where Dave and I had lived for so long.

In an offhand way, Katherine mentioned that she'd run into Arlene, an exuberant Christian woman who used to clean our house when Dave and I were too busy with work (and in my case, drinking) to do things like dust. My sister described how she'd told Arlene how "neat it was" that I'd admitted I was an alcoholic and went to treatment.

I couldn't believe my ears. "You what!?" I said. "You told *Arlene*? Who said you could do that?! She's going to tell the whole entire town!"

"I thought you didn't mind who knew!" she responded. "You seemed so positive about it, and I knew Arlene would be happy for you."

It was true that when I revealed my secret, I'd framed it in the most positive terms possible. But I'd done so mainly in order to hide how embarrassed I was. And while I hadn't sworn anyone to secrecy, I had assumed that people would respect my privacy.

Now, I was certain that news of my alcoholism was being broadcast far and wide to former neighbors, coworkers, and acquaintances. Not because Arlene lacked integrity, but because she wasn't even told to keep the news a secret. Plus, gossip travels fast in that small town, especially when it can be couched in terms of Christian caring and concern.

The thought of it made me want to punch my sister right through the phone.

Later that night, I vented to Dave about her indiscretion, leaving out the part about how genuinely sorry she was. He shared my dismay, but not my sustained wrath.

Two days later, when I was still having fantasies of ripping my sister's hair out by the roots like I used to when we were little, I realized that there was more going on with me than righteous indignation. What I'd been trying to forget, and what Katherine couldn't have known, was that Arlene had found empty wine and beer bottles hidden in odd places when she cleaned our house.

Mortified, I'd been quick to blame Noah. "I can't believe he did that!" I told Arlene. "I'm so worried about his drinking."

Now, I knew that Arlene would make the connection and think: *What kind of supposedly Christian mother uses her kids as a scapegoat that way?*

Obviously, the reason I was so angry at Katherine was that I was so ashamed of myself. And so far as other people in town learning my secret, wasn't the bigger issue that I'd lost control of the telling? Unlike at my nephew's wedding, where I could manage the story and manipulate how it was received, now I was powerless to control what people thought of me.

What had seemed like an okay price to pay when I was desperate to get sober—having tons of people know about my secret drinking—now struck me as completely unacceptable.

Before I got into treatment, I knew that my ego had necessarily been smashed, my pride crushed completely. But what I failed to notice now was that, like a monster in an old B movie, it had sprung back to life. And now it was outraged that my image was being tarnished.

At the same time, it also took one look around the rooms of recovery and brightened. Here was a new arena in which to strive, achieve, and excel. If I had to be a recovering alcoholic, then I would be the best drunk who no longer drinks that you ever saw.

Not that I'd have to work hard at that, mind you. A higher power? The steps? I couldn't figure out what all the hullabaloo was about. Heck, I'd already taken most of them in my head.

I was way ahead of this game before I even began.

Secretly, I wished there was a head-start aspect to this program where you could qualify for sober time ahead of actually getting it. Like when you apply for credit, they could check your background and know you're good for it. At five months, I imagined I was more like someone with two years.

I understood why people like Nicole might need a lot of extra help. She's a chronic relapser. But I already knew I wasn't going to drink again. Ever.

ගි

In late August, Dave and I made plans to fly to Oregon to visit our grown kids, four of whom were living in the Portland area. I couldn't wait to show off my new sober self. I was pretty sure my kids would notice a difference, a palpable peace and serenity about me. I'd be less self-centered, loud, and obnoxious, which I had long suspected were words that described my inebriated personality.

I was especially anxious to impress Noah. And my plan was pretty simple. Noah would notice how happy I was (I was determined to look happy), and then he'd want what I had (even though I still wasn't always sure that I did), and then he'd want to get sober, too.

And we'd all live happily ever after.

ॐ

Our second evening in Portland, a whole gang of us (our kids and their friends) went to see my stepson Taylor's band perform in a groovy bar. Promising Dave that we wouldn't have a repeat of the wine-like-rose-petals fiasco, I insisted that he go ahead and have a beer with his kids. Otherwise, it would look like I was not *letting* him drink, the opposite of the image I wanted to project.

Privately, I dreaded the whole ordeal. I figured all the kids would be watching me to see how long my eyes lingered on their own golden, foamy beers. And there I'd be, sucking on a Perrier, trying not to fantasize about someone accidently slipping in a shot of vodka.

Remember to smile, I told myself. *Don't let on that you feel deprived.*

I didn't count on Dave's ex-wife showing up. Don't get me wrong—Deb is a lovely person, and our relationship has always been amicable. One year, Dave and I even joined her and her husband for Christmas dinner at their house in Portland, along with all the kids.

But tonight, something about her being there bugged me. Why did she have to come? She'd already seen Taylor play in his band. She lived in his town. Good grief, couldn't she just give us this one night without having to be part of it?

Disturbed, I went to the ladies' room to gather myself, wishing for the days when my purse contained the answer to my social anxiety. When I returned to the bar a few minutes later, the table where everyone was sitting together was too crowded. I found a stool against a wall where I had a good view of the show (and our table).

I couldn't help but notice that Deb was making herself the center of attention (wasn't that where I was supposed to be?). And something about the way she sipped her wine (or maybe the fact that she could) annoyed the heck out of me. When the kids and Dave tried to get me to join them, scooting to make room, I resisted.

The longer we stayed, the harder it became to sustain the hard work of pretending not to pout. As the night dragged on, I knew I'd begun to glower. But no one seemed to notice or care. They all kept smiling, focused on the band, on Taylor, and on enjoying one another.

Imagine that.

By the time the night was over, I was convinced that if I could have had just one drink to loosen me up, I would have enjoyed the evening. I would have been sitting with everyone and feeling included. I would have been funny and witty and, I was quite certain, even enjoyed Deb's company.

Later, what dismayed me the most about the evening wasn't that I didn't get to drink, or that Deb was there, or that I felt left out. It was that I had blown my opportunity to impress everyone—Noah in particular—with my newfound serenity.

ᔥ

I'd get one more chance, at least with Noah. The next stop on our trip was the Oregon coast, where Dave and I had rented a house. We had invited the kids to drive over from Portland to stay when they could. At times, the house felt a little like a hostel with people coming and going.

On the second day, we went crabbing in a small motorboat, which was a beloved family tradition. We did a lot of whooping with excitement every time we finally caught a male crab that measured big enough to keep. Later, we cleaned the crab while listening to music. In the old days, I would have been in heaven cracking the shells and digging out the meat with an increasingly sticky glass of Chardonnay nearby.

Now, it was just work.

After dinner, we played poker with pennies. The boys, as usual, drank a fair amount of beer. As usual, I got a little competitive. In the heat of playing to win, I forgot to even notice or care that I was supposed to be a different person now—sober, spiritually minded, a poster child for recovery.

Finally, toward the end of a high stakes round of Texas Hold 'Em, Noah announced, "I can't believe it, Mom! You haven't changed at all. If anything, you're worse now than when you were drinking."

Nathan laughed. "Mom, this just proves that you weren't a brat because you were drinking," he said. "This is the real you!"

Their comments stung, but I tried not to let them see how much. Later, as we headed off to bed, I suddenly understood.

I had naïvely assumed that when I got sober, a better Heather would naturally emerge. For the past decade, I had chalked up much, if not most, of my bad behaviors to my drinking. But clearly, alcohol hadn't created my personality flaws, it only exacerbated and magnified them.

⑨

During the final part of our stay in Oregon, Dave and I attended a writer's conference at a nearby hotel. Our room had a minibar.

If you're a drunk like me, when you're alone in a hotel room

117

and you know your husband is not coming back soon, the minibar comes to life. Those tiny, chilled bottles with a slight wet film on them start pleading with you to unscrew their metal caps. After a while, it becomes hard to explain why you shouldn't have a swill of vodka. That's what those little fridges are for. *You're supposed to use them. It's part of what you're paying for!*

I made it through, but barely.

And there were other close calls. At the beach, Dave had gone to the store for dinner one afternoon and left me home alone. I knew that there were all these beers left in the fridge from the night before. I knew no one had counted them or would notice if I drank a couple. The opportunity screamed at me even as I let the chance fly by and drank a Diet Coke.

Later, when I thought back on our trip, I was surprised to realize that my greatest moments of temptation had little to do with alcohol, and everything to do with wanting to *sneak*. It was the idea of getting *away* with something that I couldn't resist. I missed the rush of adrenaline I used to feel when I thought that I was secretly winning some game no one else was even smart enough to play.

No wonder many of my most vivid childhood memories involve sneaking, cheating, or lying. Throughout elementary school, I spent my milk money every day at the corner grocery on candy. I can't count all the times I carefully snuck into our kitchen cupboard to steal a Ding Dong from a box that was strictly meant for school lunches only.

I often cheated at games with my siblings. I remember playing some weird card game called Guts with my brother Jim and a friend of his named Blake. My friend Teresa and I were partners against the boys, and we worked out an elaborate system of signals and code that involved pressing each other's toes under the table in order to win.

Every couple hours, Blake would go back home and get more money. And Teresa and I would ride our bikes down to the corner store and buy more snacks. Soda, Laffy Taffy, and big bags of Cheetos, which we ate in front of my brother and his friend.

I thoroughly enjoyed myself, and I didn't fess up to my brother until I was in my twenties.

I thought my behavior was normal. I thought everyone lived this way. I'm sure part of my learning early to lie, cheat, and steal had to do with growing up in a very dysfunctional, screaming, fighting family where it was every man for himself.

Every day I woke up ready to get mine, ready to win, prepared to beat out my siblings for anything good (the TV, the best spot on the couch, the last of the bread for toast).

One of my earliest memories of drinking was when at age twelve I somehow got hold of a twelve-pack of beer. I hated the taste, but even then, it was all about how they made me feel. I drank the warm beers in my bedroom, carefully rationing them. Then I hid the empties all over the basement family room until I could dispose of the cans properly.

At twelve, I was already in training to be a secret drunk.

And I knew how to blame-shift, too. Hide the foil wrapper from the pilfered Ding Dong in the couch cushions instead of putting it in the garbage. Arrange the remaining Ding Dongs in the box just right, so that no one notices until later that one is missing. And then, when it becomes obvious to the family that we're one Ding Dong short for school lunches, accuse your brother. *Vehemently.* Once the accusations start to fly, conveniently "find" the wrapper in the cushion and confront your brother with the proof of his crime.

This kind of premeditated trickery repeated itself with Dave. It wasn't enough to just sneak alcohol. I had to make Dave think I was drinking less than him.

Often, on a hot Saturday afternoon in the summer, Dave and I would open a six-pack of beer while sitting out in the yard. I'd run in the house to use the bathroom, guzzle my can in under a minute, then replace it with a full beer from my stash, which would contain the same size and brand beer, because I planned ahead.

In this way, I'd have maybe four beers down, still pretending to be on my first, before Dave opened a second.

At which point, I'd say to Dave, "Is that your *second* beer!? You're getting way ahead of me!"

I know. Rotten. How did I not hate myself?

But I did hate myself. Thoroughly. But hating myself only made me want to drink more. And then I hated myself more.

Thus the vicious cycle.

ᔕ

On the flight home from Oregon, I tried to reassure myself that the trip had been a rousing success, even if no one was as impressed as I hoped. At least I had proven that I could handle temptation. If I could resist the seductions of a minibar, and if I could manage to ignore beer in the fridge while in an empty house, then I probably had this thing whipped.

I get it. I got it. I have it.

Right.

• fourteen •

DRINKING AT DAVE

When I was drinking, I used to have a lot of nightmares wherein I was frantic for a drink but couldn't manage to get my hands on alcohol. I'd start doing desperate things, taking wild chances, at which point the dream would shift into a nightmare as Dave caught me red-handed trying to hide an enormous pile of bottles behind the toaster, or under the couch cushions.

I'd wake up sweaty, scared, and thirsty.

After I quit drinking, the nature of my nightmares changed. Now they typically featured the horror of accidentally drinking alcohol, not realizing what I was doing until it was too late. I'd be totally devastated about the relapse, debating whether to lie or not, when I'd wake up and realize with great relief, *I didn't really relapse!*

A couple weeks shy of my six-month sobriety mark, I had my worst nightmare yet. But I wasn't sleeping.

☙

Over the years, Dave and I had always loved to visit New York City. We'd start with beers at a sidewalk café in the late afternoon. Then we'd shift to pubs, eating appetizers with our gin and tonics. Eventually, it was time for a late dinner with wine, often followed by a nightcap (and for me, more secret drinking in the hotel bathroom before bed).

In mid-September, a year after I'd first met Susan at her wedding, she and Larry invited Dave and me to join them in New York to celebrate their first anniversary. Susan had a friend whose apartment we could all rent dirt cheap for a week.

It sounded like a perfect plan. Knowing I'd be with another recovering alcoholic was a comfort and added to my confidence. I'd have Susan for support. But since Larry was a normal drinker and liked a glass of red wine with dinner—you guessed it—I told Dave to drink a wee bit of wine in the evenings with poor Larry.

Initially, Dave resisted the idea. He only drank these days on very rare occasions. Now, he again reminded me of the wine-like-rose-petals incident.

I was indignant. Outraged, even. "I've come so far since then. I'm way past that. I can handle it!"

Finally, he agreed.

Just as I predicted, I didn't have a problem. At least at first. However, as the week unfolded, it seemed like Dave sipped a little bit more wine each evening. Midweek, dinner took a long time to unfold, so I didn't mind when he drank half of a second glass. After dinner with Susan and Larry, we met up with an old friend from Oregon who wanted to go to a wine bar. Dave had part of a third glass.

Still, I was just fine. So there.

Meanwhile, I had planned to go to some meetings with Susan while we were in New York. But the four of us had so many cool things to do, like attend the Summer of Love exhibit at the Guggenheim or stroll through Central Park or the Natural Science Museum. It never seemed like the right time for a recovery meeting.

Susan offered to go with me, but I could tell it wasn't a big deal to her, and she was mostly trying to accommodate me. Didn't she realize that I was a big girl now? I wasn't pining for alcohol just because I had less time in sobriety than her (Susan was about eight years sober to my five-plus months). If she could go a week without a meeting, I could, too.

On the final night of our trip, we took Susan and Larry out to belatedly celebrate their one-year anniversary. Dave conferred with Larry and then he ordered a bottle of wine. *Okay,* I thought. *Special occasion. This is all about the anniversary. And probably, he and Larry don't plan to finish it off.*

I was pleased when Dave also ordered a bottle of expensive sparkling water for Susan and me. We deserved something special just for us.

After both bottles arrived at the table, Dave poured us girls our sparkling water in our wineglasses, like a gentleman should. But then, he also poured our water into his and Larry's empty water glasses, too—like it was regular water. This went on throughout the evening. While he and Larry drank the wine, he ordered another bottle of sparkling water, continuing to use it like tap water for himself and Larry.

The outrage! The insensitivity! Later, I would continue to maintain that it was the *water* that put me over the edge.

However, I didn't freak out right away. I had my dignity. And there was too little privacy for me to spew the kind of anger I was brewing. So that night, I simply gave Dave the cold shoulder. Let him wonder. When he inquired about my mood, I knew that he *knew.* He had to know I was pissed about the wine and the water. How dare he act confused or concerned when he obviously didn't give a rat's behind?!

The next day, in the cab on the way to the airport, I hinted at the source of my outrage. Even though we were relatively alone, and the driver seemed distracted, I still couldn't come out and tell Dave precisely why I was so angry, because I knew it would sound stupid—"You ordered a whole bottle of wine—and then you finished it!—and then you drank our water, too!"

So, apart from some nasty, whispered remarks that I refused to elaborate on, my huff continued onto the plane, where again we had no privacy. Fortunately, we had an hour-long layover in Minneapolis in which to talk and, hopefully, make up. I imagined that Dave couldn't wait to find a quiet corner where he could tell me that he loved me and he understood why I'd be mad, and he'd beg me to forgive him.

Instead, as soon as we deplaned in Minneapolis, Dave suggested that we go our separate ways and meet back up at the next gate. He said he was tired of my glaring at him.

What a jerk! He walked toward a news store and I stormed off in the opposite direction, fuming. *He knows I'm angry and hurting. He knows this is a dangerous time for me. He knows I might drink. Obviously, he doesn't care!*

I found a bar and marched in, determined to drink *at* Dave, as they say. I sat up at the bar next to a couple of men who were watching football on one screen and baseball on another. I ordered a Chardonnay. I felt paranoid, though, like the guy next to me *knew* I was a drunk who shouldn't be drinking.

As I thought of my fellow alcoholics and my fondness for them, a wave of hesitation hit me hard. What about Nicole? How would I explain this? She was the one who periodically relapsed, not me. I felt like Judas, betraying her with a sip instead of a kiss. Then, I realized that it wasn't too late. I could still stop. I didn't have to go through with it.

But then the bartender brought my glass, and it was enormous and nearly full. Like a sign from...well, a sign, anyway. So I tried to enjoy it. I tried to *really* taste it. I tried to have that *Ahhh, finally!* feeling about it. But somehow, it just didn't taste like I remembered. It didn't slide smoothly down my throat like liquid gold. It was sour and cutting and a bit vinegary.

Soon, my cheeks started to feel numb. I finished the glass quickly and ordered another. Now that I'd blown it, I might as well, right?

I drank the second glass and paid the bill. Then I put some spearmint gum in my mouth and went to meet Dave at the gate. When he approached, I glared at him and made some smart remark. For some reason, he was suspicious. He asked if I'd been drinking.

"Of course not!" I said, as if this was an outrageous question. "How could you even ask such a thing?"

Once we got onto the plane, I changed my mind. I wasn't drunk *enough*. The whole point was that I wanted Dave to know that I was drinking. The goal was to hurt and punish him by chucking my sobriety, which I knew was precious to him.

As soon as the flight attendant with the drink cart came down the aisle, I was ready. I dug in my purse for money. I had Dave's attention now, since back then you still only had to pay for alcohol, never water, coffee, or soda. But still, he must have doubted that I'd do it.

Finally the attendant reached our row. "Would you like anything to drink?" she asked.

"Yes, I'll have a glass of white wine," I announced, reaching my arm over Dave to hand her my bills.

"What are you doing?!" Dave said to me, obviously alarmed.

"I'm having a drink. Do you *mind*?"

The flight attendant hesitated, but then she poured my drink. I flipped down the tray table and placed the cup and small bottle in front of me. I started to sip it slowly.

Dave put his elbow on the armrest between us and held his hand up near his face, I guessed so that he wouldn't have to watch.

While I downed the wine, salty tears slipped down my face and ran into my wineglass, and I drank them.

§

Sometime later, I ran across a story that perfectly captured the insanity of my determination to drink at Dave.

It was a piece about how a woman in Texas took revenge on her ex-boyfriend because he took back some jewelry he'd given her. She broke into his home while he was gone and stole his pet goldfish. When the guy discovered them missing, he alerted police. The cops arrived at the girlfriend's house just in time to see that she'd fried the goldfish and eaten all but one.

My first reaction was horror: *What was she thinking?! Why would she do that to herself?* If she wanted to punish the ex-boyfriend, she should have tricked him into eating his own fish. Or simply left them in the frying pan for him to see.

And then it dawned on me. This was the exact kind of insanity that I'd suffered in the Minneapolis Airport. I had thought, *Take that, buster!*

But *I* was the one who ate the fish.

§

That night, when we got home from the airport, Dave and I didn't speak. I wanted more wine (after the wine-like-rose-petals fiasco, we'd disposed of the big red jug in the laundry room closet). How stupid was I that I hadn't had the foresight to save at least one small emergency bottle in case this day came?

I went to bed in the guest room that night for the first time since I'd gotten sober. I sobbed and raged like a twelve-year-old. It was just like the old days.

The following morning, Dave had to go to work. Later, I went out and bought a bottle of wine for that evening, just in case our argument didn't get resolved to my satisfaction when Dave got home.

And what would have been to my satisfaction? Dave saying all the right things: "I understand why you felt that way…" "I was wrong…" "I'm so sorry…" I had a pretty good script prepared for him. As long as he stuck to it pretty much word for word, we'd be fine.

Dave didn't. Couldn't. And by now a part of me was so angry at myself for drinking that I didn't want to come back down to reality yet. I might as well *keep* drinking, since I was going to have to change my sobriety date anyway.

When Dave got home, I managed to be unreasonable and defiant. Despite his valiant efforts to make up, I made reconciliation impossible. I even threw a couple shoes at our bedroom door for good measure. Confident that I was justified to keep drinking now, I stayed in my office and downed the entire bottle of wine I'd bought earlier.

Six months ago, a single bottle would have felt like a drop in the bucket. But now that I'd been sober for a while, it knocked me for a loop. I woke up hungover and sick with regret and misery. I felt like I was coming out of a nightmare that I'd had no control over. *How did this happen?*

When Dave got home from work that second night, I could tell he was extremely hurt and angry. I could also tell that the balance had shifted, in terms of who was the more aggrieved party. Clearly, I'd gone way too far.

This time, I approached him to make apologies. We talked quietly. I was finally reasonable. I was finally done drinking. Again.

He told me that he'd lain awake in bed the night before and cried. His admission felt like a dagger to my heart. I was filled with sincere remorse—horrified by what I'd done and how I'd treated him. I begged Dave to forgive me, and he did.

But it wasn't that simple. It wasn't like in the old days when this kind of terrible fight was par for the course. Now, something about my relapse and the subsequent arguments that followed had re-opened old wounds.

Up to now, my husband had largely refrained from expressing anger as he gradually learned the whole truth about the past twelve years. I think he didn't want to rock the boat or take risks with my sobriety. And despite my assurances, I think he didn't believe that it was safe to express anger at me without fear of ret-ribution.

All that changed with my relapse.

PART THREE

• fifteen •

AFTERMATH

hadn't expected that getting sober a second time would be harder than the first. I had only drank for two evenings, after all. And yet, reintroducing alcohol to my system, combined with feeling guilt and remorse, made the next few months much harder than I could have ever dreamed.

This time, I didn't have that giddy feeling of making a new start. I didn't have the protective walls of a treatment center. And now, I had planted the idea in the back of my mind that relapse was an option. I hated that.

But what I hated even more was how Minneapolis and its aftermath provided Dave with painful, visceral reminders of what life used to be like on a regular basis.

In the days following our return, we did a lot of talking. We took Edmund on walks he wasn't asking for. We had work to do, because what we had taken for granted now seemed fragile and tenuous. And even though we had patched things up, Dave's anger kept tumbling out at odd moments, often taking both of us by surprise.

One day we were driving up I-25 when something I said about his friend Larry triggered a memory. He asked me, "Do you remember that time we got in a horrible fight simply because Larry and I had had a couple beers in the afternoon while you were working?"

I did. Back in his single days, Larry had driven up from LA to central Oregon to visit us. The day after he arrived, he and Dave had sat in a Thai restaurant and had a couple beers. Later, when Dave and I were alone in the car, I tore into him for drinking "without me." Stung by my attack, Dave lost his temper, pulling the car off to the side of the road so he could yell at me without killing us both.

I used his reaction to throw even more fuel on the fire.

That night, the tension in the house was too much for Larry. He turned around and drove all the way back to California.

Now the memory filled me with shame and disbelief. "What I did was outrageous," I told Dave. "So unfair to you and Larry. I'm so, so sorry."

A few days later we were out to dinner, and I said—almost as a throwaway—how relieved I was to not have my purse packed with alcohol. The comment was innocent, I thought, and hopeful. But it sparked something for Dave. "You used me as your alcohol pimp," he said bitterly.

"Your what?" I asked.

"If we were anywhere but home, it was up to me to make sure you had access to alcohol by five o'clock—or look out!"

He was right. Even if I had alcohol in my purse, I had needed to drink some kind of alcohol in front of Dave, too—in case he kissed me and smelled alcohol on my breath. But it was worse than that. By four or five o'clock, I had expected him to act like *he* wanted something to drink, too. If he said, "Do we need to stop somewhere so you can have a beer?" I got highly offended. That wasn't how our game was supposed to be played.

And there was anger surrounding his mother, too. Our trips to Portland, which usually included a stop to visit her, had always bristled with tension. "What was I thinking?" he said sarcastically. "We couldn't possibly stop to visit my poor, lonely mother in her assisted-living apartment at five o'clock at night. They don't serve *wine* at the assisted-living center! And God knows Heather can't make it another hour, especially if she's supposed to pretend to enjoy the visit!"

He was right about that one, too. Without enough to drink, I had found it hard to even *pretend* to be interested in other people.

Although neither of us liked these conversations, we knew they were important. We hadn't been able to process Dave's anger the first time around, but this time I think we realized we had no choice.

Eventually, we were able to discuss drinking-related injuries from our past without becoming alienated from one another in the present. We were ready now, too, to see how some of Dave's own hurtful past behaviors in our marriage (he wasn't perfect, after all) had stemmed in part from his suppressed anger at me.

One day, it dawned on us that Dave was in recovery, too. Not from alcoholism, but from being married to a duplicitous, raging drunk.

§

I'm telling you first about what changed with Dave after I drank at him. But that wasn't the only thing that changed and, in terms of staying sober, not the most important. The third day after our return, I did what I knew I needed to do and dreaded doing with all my heart.

I walked myself back into a meeting. When the chairperson asked the routine question, "Is there anyone here with less than thirty days of sobriety?" I raised my hand, my face red with embarrassment.

By now, I had also broken the news about my relapse to Nicole. At first, she lit up. Suddenly she had more days of continuous sobriety than me. Then she said, "That's no fair! You got to drink. I'm so jealous."

"That's *exactly* the kind of thinking that got me drunk again," I told her. "Trust me, I didn't enjoy a single minute of it." And this, I realized, was true. I'd been miserable while I drank, and now I was miserable about having drunk. For the umpteenth time since New York, I asked myself, *How could I have let this happen?*

Really, the answer was obvious and I knew it. I had assumed that being a Christian and having such a supportive husband gave me a leg up on your average drunk. I thought this meant that I didn't have to work as hard as other people. I hadn't felt the need to actually take the steps. Or get a sponsor.

Once, when I got tired of people asking me if I had one, I had approached a nice lady I didn't know and we had coffee. I called her my sponsor, and told my friends she was. But the truth is that after our one meeting, she went off to Thailand, and I never saw her again.

Why had I imagined that I was on a path of spiritual transformation when I refused to take the simple steps suggested as the primary means to change?

This time around, I realized I needed to go all in. *Duh.*

Within a week of my relapse, I hesitantly asked a woman named Kate if she would consider sponsoring me and helping me take the steps. She seemed delighted to oblige.

Kate was pretty, blonde, and slightly older than me. She had a reputation as a tough cookie. I knew that she'd helped many women to get and stay sober. More than a few of these, including Nicole, had specifically recommended her as a sponsor. "I don't get why you don't ask Kate," Nicole kept saying. "You guys seem a lot alike."

But I'd been determined to ask anybody *but* Kate. Now I knew the reason why. *She had never seemed at all impressed by me.*

In other words, she was probably the perfect match.

§

My assignment for step one was simple. Kate asked me to write out my entire drinking history. The idea was to help me see—in case I didn't already—how unmanageable my drinking had become, and to remove any doubt in my mind that I was an alcoholic.

The last thing I expected was to be surprised by my own story. But I was. Something about writing it out made the misery and the heartache of those years more real to me. I wept as I wrote about one of the greatest losses of my drinking career—something I had never before admitted to anyone. It was a baby that I never had.

When Dave and I got married, I was just thirty. I still had plenty of time for a baby, and I knew I wanted one with Dave. I knew that we'd be one of those couples with his, hers, and *ours*. I was so madly in love with Dave, I adored the idea of having his baby. And Dave was completely open. Every now and then he'd say, "Let's do it. Let's have a baby!"

But as desperately as I wanted to share this experience with him, I couldn't imagine going nine months without a drink. I was terrified of getting pregnant, drinking in secret, and having a baby with fetal alcohol syndrome. Every year, I told myself that I would quit drinking next year, then try to get pregnant.

As I approached forty, I finally realized that a baby wasn't ever going to happen, and I let that sweet dream die. Of course, I kept right on drinking.

Now I admitted to myself that my fear of going without a drink was also why I dissuaded Dave when he wanted us to join his siblings in Africa for a big family reunion. And it was why I had purchased tickets for him and his daughter to go see his son, Taylor, when he was living in China. Without constant access to alcohol, I couldn't go with him, so I made sure Jana could.

When I'd finished writing out my drinking history, Kate asked me to come to her house. We met in a small upstairs room where she worked with all of her sponsees. I was sort of in awe. What would that be like, to help so many women? To be entrusted with so much shame, pain, and loss? To give so much of your life and time away like that for free?

She had me read aloud to her what I'd written. It was ten pages, typed—every page crushing proof of my bondage to alcohol. Even though nothing I read seemed all that dramatic—no arrests, jail time, emergency rooms, or wrecked cars—it stunned me to hear my story told aloud in my own voice to another person.

It was the story of a woman I had never imagined could be me.

Afterward, we talked through step two. Did I believe God could restore me to sanity? Kate wanted to know.

I balked. Restore me to sanity? "But I'm not insane!" I protested. And wasn't using this word somehow politically incorrect? Wasn't it an insult to people who actually were crazy? Having a mentally ill father made me think I should be sensitive about this, or at least pretend to be.

Kate explained that in recovery we define *insanity* as "doing the same thing over and over while expecting different results." She also explained that *insanity* is a very useful term for the kind of irrational and crazy thinking that alcoholics indulge in when they let their minds run wild and don't work the program.

By those definitions, she was definitely talking about me. I had allowed the insanity of alcoholism to return to my thinking long before I took that drink in the Minneapolis airport.

"It was like I was already drunk," I told Kate. "Otherwise, I would not have done it."

She nodded. She explained to me again something I'd heard before and would have told you that I knew. That sobriety isn't the same thing as not drinking. You can be as dry as the Gobi Desert and still be a slave to alcoholic thinking.

"So, yes," I told Kate. "I believe that God can restore me to sanity."

Next question. Was I ready to turn my will and life over to the care of God as I understood Him?

It was hard not to smirk. "I'm pretty sure I've already done that," I told her. I explained about my Christian background, how I had turned my life over to God eons ago, not to mention the many times since that I'd rededicated my life to God in some way or another.

Kate didn't seem fazed. She came from a Christian background, too, she said. But recovery wasn't about religion. It's not about what you do or don't believe about the Bible, she said. It's about giving control of your life to God every day and trusting Him to keep you sober.

"Are you ready to do that?" she asked. "Are you convinced that Heather is powerless to do this on her own?"

I nodded, mute.

Together we got on our knees and prayed. It was a short but heartfelt prayer of surrender, of peeling my fingers off my own life. I asked God to relieve me of the bondage of self, and I committed to seeking his will instead of mine.

Walking down the steps of Kate's house to my car, I felt hopeful for the first time in a long time. I felt saved all over again—this time from myself.

sixteen

GOD AS I DON'T UNDERSTAND HIM

'll admit, when I first got into recovery, it shocked me to see God clearly at work in the lives of people who didn't call him by the "right" name or necessarily identify themselves as Christians. I didn't quite approve. I guessed that in any given meeting, at least a third of the people wouldn't dream of darkening the steps of a church.

I remember thinking, *Maybe I can help some of these clearly confused people get a better, more biblical grip on God.*

But ever since my relapse, I wondered how strong my grip really was—more to the point, *what good it did me.* After all, having darkened the steps of church for decades myself hadn't kept me from ending up a hopeless drunk, had it?

In the days following that prayer in Kate's upstairs room, it dawned on me that I was trapped in a vise of cynicism and arrogance.

On the one hand, I was deeply disillusioned about a Christian faith that hadn't been able to save me from alcohol. Why should I believe that the same God who almost let me drown once would rescue me now and into the future?

On the other hand, ironically, I assumed that my Christian background qualified me as a spiritual expert. If what I'd been told was true—that alcoholism is a spiritual problem that requires a spiritual solution—I was good to go. I had God in my back pocket.

Now, my pockets seemed empty.

Something about the way I approached God wasn't working—maybe had never worked. Which meant I had a problem. I knew now that I couldn't hope to stay sober without fixing my relationship with God. But the God I thought I knew and understood was not the God who could save me.

I needed to find God as I *didn't* understand him, or I was doomed.

§

One rainy day in October, a couple weeks after my relapse, I was tempted to stay home from my usual noon meeting—the one in the room with the bullet hole in the door and the white plastic chairs. But on the off chance that someone might say something I needed to hear, I dragged myself downtown.

I was trying to practice a new willingness to learn from people I might have disregarded in the past.

People like Miguel.

I didn't recognize him as a regular, but he would have blended into the usual crowd. He was Hispanic, midtwenties, small in stature, and handsome in a sweet way.

"My name is Miguel," he said, "and I'm an alcoholic."

In halting English he told everyone how grateful he was to God that he was sober and free. Before he came to these meetings, he explained, he never used to pray or go to church. "I didn't have good ideas of God," he said.

He went on to tell us that he worked construction, where everyone drank and did drugs. He used to do the same, often using the on-site port-a-potty to smoke marijuana and slug hard liquor.

"But not anymore," he said. He still spends time in the port-a-potty, but now he goes there to beg God to help him stay sober. "There's a tiny mirror on the inside of the door of the port-a-potty," he said. "I go and look at me in the mirror every day and I say, 'Miguel, you no want to drink or do drugs! Think about your wife! Think about your baby!'"

Around the circle, laughter broke out at the absurd picture of Miguel scolding himself in an outhouse mirror. But Miguel wanted to press his point home. "I make you laugh, maybe," he said, "but the port-a-potty is my sanctuary. My name is Miguel, and I am an alcoholic."

And I had come so close to skipping this meeting.

Later, reflecting on what Miguel said, I realized it hadn't once occurred to me to wonder exactly which God Miguel was referring to. Or if the God of his understanding matched up with mine.

It seemed wrong to ask or even care.

꩜

I began bumping into Miguels everywhere—people who had just enough awareness of God to know they were desperate for his help. And lately I couldn't help noticing that not only did God seem to be helping these folks recover, but in many cases they spoke as if they depended on him in a more literal way than I ever had. I was tempted to conclude that they had more confidence in God's grace and goodness than I did.

But how could that possibly be?

I could have very quickly outlined a Bible study about God's attributes for Miguel or anyone else in those rooms, while most of them would have been clueless about the passages I cited, how to find them, and how to make the complex leaps of logic required to get their theology straight.

So why did I want what Miguel and so many others here had?

᭍

Turns out, I wasn't the only one who noticed something different about these people. Even before my relapse, Dave had begun to join me at some of my meetings where visitors were welcome. At first, he came mainly to support me. I loved how he always introduced himself: "I'm Dave, and I'm here with Heather." But soon he insisted that he got as much out of these meetings as anyone.

One of our favorite meetings took place on the top floor of an old Catholic hospital. If you looked past the potted plastic trees, the room offered breathtaking views of Pikes Peak. The hour-long format was simple. A visiting speaker would tell his or her story for twenty minutes and suggest a topic for discussion. Then people would share.

It sounds so simple. Boring, even. Yet, time and again, Dave and I left that room shaking our heads in wonder. How could it be that a support group for alcoholics and addicts could feel so much like a close encounter with grace? Why did it seem like God showed up here more visibly than He did at most of the churches we had attended?

One day, in the middle of this meeting and while gazing out the window, I heard yet another recovering drunk echoing Miguel's story almost point for point: "I was desperate. I cried out for help, and God answered me. Now I rely on Him every day to keep me sober."

And something clicked. It was about the difference in how we had arrived at our faith.

Most of the people in this room had come to faith in the *op-*

posite way that I had. They brought nothing with them, and they knew it. Desperate, they leaned in faith on a God they didn't understand—a God many could not even name—to keep them sober. As this God-as-they-understood-him proved faithful, they came to conclusions about who he was and why they should trust him for another day.

In stark contrast, I brought a finely tuned and biblically supported belief system about God. Sometimes I acted on those beliefs. More often than not, though, I was pretty sure that just having them—being "right" in what I believed—constituted the greater part of the spiritual life.

I had strutted into the rooms of recovery as Little Miss Christian, smug owner of the answer book. But they had walked in like cripples leaning on canes.

I looked out at the Rockies and sighed. *I don't have something to teach them,* I thought to myself. *They have something to teach me.* Like how to lean—helplessly, foolishly, hopefully—on a God you can't fully explain.

And how to do it, over and over, every day.

๑

Working with Kate, I started to see how my Christian background had in many ways actually inoculated me against spiritual growth. For decades, I had heard the same truths over and over in a language that had become so familiar that everything I heard rang of something I thought I already knew.

That meant that for years, deep spiritual truths I heard in church had bounced off of me like a rubber ball off cement.

How far back had everything I knew so well in my head stopped making it through to my heart? A decade of working in Christian publishing—where so much emphasis is placed on making sure every doctrinal dot is perfectly connected—probably hadn't helped.

Regardless of when or where it started, I had mistaken a belief-based faith for an experience-based faith. I'd been on a prideful intellectual journey aimed at being right about God instead of on a desperate soul journey aimed at being real with God.

The difference can make you sick.

For too long, that third-step invitation—to turn our lives over to the care of God "as we understood him"—had struck me as vaguely suspicious. Now it hinted at a promise. What if I could find a new understanding of God, and a new way to approach him, that had little in common with the old way?

What if I could rediscover God *as I didn't understand him*—and arrive somewhere closer to the truth?

For a while that fall, I wondered if recovery alone might constitute this new spiritual path. After all, Dave and I hadn't yet been able to find a church home in the Springs. Maybe we could just quit looking altogether and get our spiritual needs met through recovery meetings.

I loved the idea of sleeping in on Sunday mornings and never having to sit through another dull sermon.

But this brilliant idea didn't last. Deep in my heart, I knew that God wasn't calling me away from my faith to recovery, or away from recovery to my faith. Instead, I sensed I was being invited to walk forward in the sometimes scary tension I felt between the two.

My path in recovery and my path as a Christ follower didn't have to be in conflict. They could illumine and inform one another. Like streetlamps lining both sides of the street, they could light my way back to God.

ᔑ

It was around this time that I began to read books about the spirituality of recovery in addition to those prescribed by my program. Now that I recognized how little I really knew, I wanted to know more. What was it about this approach and others like it that helped people find hope when so many other avenues—jail, therapy, church—had failed?

One of the first books I picked up was *Seeds of Grace*, written by Sister Molly Monahan, a practicing Catholic nun. Like me, after she'd gotten sober, she'd become intrigued with the spiritual aspects of recovery. Also like me, she couldn't understand how someone like her (with extensive religious learning and training) had ended up a helpless drunk.

Something she said caught my attention. She wrote that she honestly believed she'd learned more of God and come closer to Him through recovery than she had during all her years of religious training. Yet she expressed bafflement at how and why this could be the case.

I skipped forward in the book, searching the part where she finds the answer. But the closest she came was her conclusion that "in my alcoholism I experienced myself as being utterly lost and unable to help (save) myself in a way that I never had before."

It wasn't the answer I thought I was looking for, but something about her observation resonated. I remembered Miguel in his port-a-potty. And I then thought back on all my years of being a Christian, including the early years after I was newly "saved." Sure, I had always known in my head that I was a sinner saved by grace.

But utterly lost? Unable to save myself?

Like the nun, I couldn't remember experiencing that kind of spiritual desperation until I admitted that I was a hopeless, helpless alcoholic. Only then did the truth of my absolute need for saving and my complete inability to save myself finally become real to me.

Up until that day when I fell on my knees and sobbed beside my bed, God's grace had been a nice option, a convenient option, but not my only option. I had known about grace, talked about grace, written about grace. Grace had been part of my rallying cry when I was mentally at war with all those horrible, legalistic Christians who obviously didn't have enough of it.

And when alcohol had taken me captive, grace had mattered to me mostly because it was a critical clause in my spiritual contract with God whereby He had to let me into heaven no matter how much I drank. I had greedily accepted the gift, only to hawk it for my drug of choice.

It was a painful epiphany with enormous implications.

Among other things, it meant that if I was ever going to experience the kind of ongoing spiritual transformation I so desperately wanted, I would have to learn the difference between ascribing to a set of Christian beliefs that had no power to change me, and clinging daily to an experience of God's love and grace that could.

ဖ

Sometimes the greatest shifts in our lives show up in the smallest ways. For me, casting all my hopes on a God I didn't understand meant learning how to set my thoughts, knowledge, and beliefs to the side. Just consciously put them all down for a spell and approach him as a spiritual pauper.

For example, I felt God inviting me to try something new and—for me—pretty radical. Something so hard that for a long time I couldn't manage to do it for more than five minutes a day.

Nothing.

God was inviting me to sit in my chair every morning with a candle and be still. Just be. Just listen. Just open my heart and stop trying to control my mind. For just a few minutes every day, stop trying to think my way out of this.

I didn't know what to expect. As my drinking had progressed, I'd mostly given up on my daily devotional reading and prayer. But now God was inviting me to get back in touch with my soul *and to bring nothing with me when I came.*

He was encouraging me to embrace the present moment, even if it contained emptiness. He was challenging me to believe the impossible—that I didn't need a substance or a thought or an activity to fill the space inside.

What I needed more was the courage to sit with the emptiness.

Being still also got me in touch with my weakness. It reminded me that I need to live in an ongoing posture of utter dependence on God. And that it's good to be pricked by pain whenever I feel the inclination toward self-reliance again.

Sitting still was teaching me that when I think I'm thirsty for a drink, what I really crave is grace, and what I need most of all in the world is God.

seventeen

THE EXACT NATURE OF MY WRONGS

I began to suspect that Nicole was lying to me. She'd been talking a great deal about going back to school, and because she had few clothes and admired mine, I'd wanted her to have some new things. So I had bought her a gift certificate to Ross, figuring that way she could get a lot for her money.

But school never happened. Even though I helped her prepare for placement tests, all it took was the math test to convince her that it was going to be too hard. Impossible, actually. Since then, the only new things she'd been wearing were bruised-looking eyes—telltale signs that she was back on meth.

I figured she had traded the gift card I'd given her for cash so she could buy drugs.

When I explained the situation to Kate, she told me kindly to mind my own business. "It sounds like you've been overinvesting in Nicole's sobriety when you should have been worrying about your own."

I knew she was right, and I knew part of the reason: I wanted to accomplish with Nicole what I had failed to do with Noah.

My getting sober had done little to impress my son with the benefits of recovery—and he didn't even know about my relapse yet. But I had become more desperate than ever to save him, or convince God to do so. Since a part of me still believed God operated by some mysterious form of quid pro quo—you give me this, I give you that—helping someone else in his place seemed like a good idea.

I guess Nicole had been that someone. God was using my worries, my failures, even my rampant good intentions to draw me toward unfinished business.

〄

Despite what happened in New York, six weeks later Dave and I still hadn't resolved the question of his occasional social drinking.

Dave approached the topic gently. There was no question in his mind that he loved having a sober life with me, he said. But when it came to his having an occasional beer or glass of wine, he felt ambivalent. He was tired of all the mixed messages, tired of being a pawn in a battle I was having with myself. He resented the idea of relying on me to grant or revoke "permission" for him to drink.

At first his words stung. I agreed that the situation was unfair, but to me the solution was obvious. Dave should just not drink. Sure, it might feel awkward now and then in social settings. But wouldn't it be worth it to protect me and our new sober life?

To Dave's credit, he was patient as we dug deeper. The issue wasn't resolved in a single conversation, but over the course of a couple weeks of discussion, a few things became clear.

For starters, I was jealous that Dave could drink like a regular person, and so I projected onto him what would be *my* experience of drinking, attaching an inordinate amount of importance and pleasure to his choice. I still felt like I was being deprived of a good thing. I knew this was a lie—and that alcohol was no longer the great purveyor of pleasure that some sick part of my brain insisted it was. But as long as this lie persisted, I would envy people who got to indulge.

Clearly, despite alcohol's absence from my body, I remained in its thrall. I was like a man who'd given up porn but still greedily gaped at every scantily clad woman he saw. This realization alarmed me. It felt like a slippery slope. And wouldn't asking Dave to abstain only further cement in my mind the lie that I was missing out on something good?

I knew the answer. And I knew that more than I wanted Dave to change, I wanted me to *be* changed. I wanted to arrive at the place where I honestly wouldn't mind if Dave drank, because drinking would no longer hold a place in my heart.

What I didn't see then was this: the fact that I *wanted* to feel differently was a sure, if small, sign that change was already taking place.

ௗ

After I had prayed the third-step prayer with Kate, she had instructed me to begin the fourth step, where a person makes "a fearless moral inventory."

"I want you to think back over your past and identify people who have hurt or offended you," she said. "We begin step four with a list of our resentments."

Thankfully, I didn't have any of those. As a Christian, I understood that we are to forgive as we have been forgiven, and I'd already generously absolved most everyone from my past. Generously—kind of like Oprah giving away cars: "And I forgive you! And I forgive you, too! And you and you…!"

When I tried to explain this to Kate, she told me to plunge ahead anyway. "List people who come to your mind even if you think you've already forgiven them," she said. "The goal isn't just forgiveness. It's to help you to recognize your part."

My part in a resentment? That didn't make sense. I figured you resented someone who had hurt or offended *you*. The very idea that someone should suggest that I had any part in the painful events of my past made me angry enough to realize that maybe I did have a few, tiny resentments tucked away in there.

Like maybe at Kate.

Still, I went home and got to work right away. By the time I got done writing, I had a long inventory of resentments. Kate had been right about how helpful it would be to write them down. But the last column of the inventory—where I needed to explain my part, where I might also be at fault—was mostly blank.

One fall afternoon in October, Kate came over to my house so we could go over my inventory together (Step 5), and surface "the exact nature of my wrongs."

She agreed with me that in many situations from childhood, I had no role or choice in what had happened. But as I grew into an adult, I became responsible for how I responded to these events. Her point echoed one I'd already heard in meetings: "When you're a child, you're a victim. But a grown-up is a volunteer."

As we talked through my list of names, a surprising thing happened. The words on the page stopped being just words. Against my will, long-buried feelings rose up in my throat. My body tightened like a spring, and my voice shook as I spoke the names of the people and events behind those words.

I couldn't find even a sliver of my former bravado.

There it was—the ugly truth. I still felt a great deal of hurt and anger about my past. It didn't matter how much counseling I'd had in my twenties, or how many times I had written about my father.

It didn't matter how much I wanted to be so over all of that. I could see now that some of the most tangled roots in my relationships were directly tied to hurts and resentments I still carried deep inside.

Some of those roots wrapped around Dave.

When I first fell in love with him, I understood that part of his appeal to me had to do with his being more mature and wise (read *fatherly*). But what I couldn't acknowledge until now was that deep down, I hoped that Dave might fix or fill the hole my father had left in my soul.

It was a setup from the get-go. I wanted Dave to be mature and fatherly, but when he was, he often became the target of the anger I really felt toward my father. His attempts to fill the empty space were doomed to come up short. It's hard to explain. When I got a little of what I wanted, I was devastated to realize how much more I needed, and then I lashed out.

A part of me knew this dynamic was true when I married Dave. But now, I began to understand how powerful it was, and how much I still felt this outsized need to get from a man what only God could give me.

Kate was helping me to see that my responses to old wounds from my past had caused new wounds to others and myself. What had started out as coping mechanisms that helped me to survive as a child had turned against me in my adult life. They had warped my instincts, bent my character, then disappeared from view.

And now, in my conversation with Kate, we were pulling them kicking and screaming into the light. Some of them I could already name.

Dishonesty. Selfish ambition. Arrogance.

§

I was beginning to understand that I needed to change in ways that went far deeper than no longer putting alcohol in my body. Just as quitting drinking hadn't changed my personality around my kids much, it hadn't fixed the person I brought to my marriage, either. That was going to take work.

But not the kind of work that began and ended with me.

That same afternoon, Kate led me through Steps 6 and 7—where I became willing to have God remove these defects of character, and then asked Him to do so.

It seemed way too easy.

Which was part of the point, of course.

Transformation wasn't going to come through my trying harder to fix myself. Scratching and clawing my way to different behavior would mostly just strengthen my ego. But neither did change have to be a once-and-for-all breakthrough, or a climactic epiphany like the kind I used to seek in the early days of my faith.

Instead, lasting change would come by patiently working a program of recovery, and by asking God to do for me what I could not do for myself.

What I needed was humility and willingness both—and not just on big occasions, but every day. Through an ongoing posture of surrender, I would be giving God access to my deepest soul while offering as little resistance as possible to His work.

This was all I had to offer.

But Kate said it was enough. And maybe it was everything.

ॐ

In the weeks ahead, I faced the daunting task of making amends to the people I had harmed.

When we are active in our addiction, most of us wreak havoc on people around us. Attempting to set things right again is an important part of the 12-step program. Step 8 is where you become willing to make amends to those you have hurt or wronged. Step 9 is where you go and make those amends directly.

This will not surprise you, but just as I thought I didn't have too much in the way of resentments, I thought I probably didn't owe many amends, either. At least, not significant ones. I mean, look at the evidence.

I laid out for Kate my superior record as a drunk: I had never sold off my own mother's prized possessions to pay for drugs. I had never drunkenly wrecked someone else's car. Or burned down a house. Broken into a pharmacy. Knocked out a spouse's teeth. Stabbed a stranger. Slept with people I couldn't name. Left a young man on a crosswalk crippled for life...

By now, I'd heard all the stories.

Kate was not persuaded. "Didn't you say that you 'got physical' with Dave?" she asked.

She had something there. I had hit someone. I hit David—hard. And kicked him. And clawed at him. I had forgotten all about that.

"And didn't you ever drive drunk with your kids in the car? Most of us did." She waited a minute, then gently continued. "And didn't you say that you spent thousands of dollars on wine that Dave didn't know about? Isn't that lying? And stealing, too?"

Now I felt really dumb. "Um. Yes. I never thought of it that way."

Obviously, I had amends to make. And I knew that once I prayed about it, and got honest with myself, that list would grow, too.

The first person I spoke to was Dave. We sat down together one evening, and one by one I listed the ways I had harmed him. It was painful for both of us. But it was made somewhat easier by the fact that I didn't have new failings to divulge this time—Dave already understood the nature of my wrongs against him.

Part of the reason we wait until Step 9 to make amends is that it takes us a while in recovery to be able to remember with clarity and see with proper perspective how we hurt others—not just by what we did, but by what we *didn't* do.

Maybe that was why I felt more trepidation about talking to my kids.

Once I got brave enough to really look at my parenting, the guilt I felt threatened to break my heart. And with both Noah and Nathan, I knew I wouldn't be able to make full amends without answering painful questions that further implicated me.

Yes, I did drive drunk with you in the car.

Yes, I did miss most of your high school sporting events—not because I wasn't there, but because I wasn't sober. I was busy drinking in the bathroom or else thinking about my next drink.

Yes, I was drinking way more than you ever could have guessed.

Yes, I lectured you about alcohol while, unknown to you, it was killing me.

Yes, every day for ten years, I betrayed your trust.

It was embarrassing, humbling, and *good*. And just as I suspected they would, both boys offered me forgiveness on the spot.

But I knew I couldn't expect such a generous reaction from everyone. I had barely begun to make amends when an author I had worked with more than once during my drinking years—we'll call him Pastor Jack—came to town and invited Dave and me to dinner.

Kate was happy for me. "What a great opportunity!" she declared. "You get to make your amends to him *in person*."

Yippee.

Honestly, I didn't think I could do it. But I was willing…if an opening presented itself.

Much to my relief, most of the dinner conversation revolved around business. Surely it would have been awkward, not to mention rude, to forcibly turn the conversation to *my* issues. This wasn't going to be the night.

Whew!

Toward the end of dinner, I visited the ladies' room. While I washed my hands, I thanked God for giving me a way out of this one, and I promised him that I'd write a really good letter to Pastor Jack soon.

When I returned to the table, Jack beamed at me as I took my seat. "Heather, I was just telling Dave how much you've changed since I saw you last. You seem so much more at peace."

The perfect opening! *Okay, God,* I thought. *Help me do this.*

I took a deep breath—and told the truth. The whole time I assisted Dave on Jack's projects, I had been leading a double life, I told him. I described for him what alcohol had done to me, and the lengths I'd gone to defend my addiction. I had guzzled 22-ounce beers while I was editing his material on the abundant life. Clearly, I had not been the helper he deserved or thought he had.

I assured him that while I didn't believe the quality of the end product had suffered, my own conscience had. I had compromised my professional and personal integrity, and I deeply regretted it.

"I lied to you every day, Jack," I said. "I cared way more about my drinking than I did about your book." I let him know I wasn't looking for easy reassurances—that wasn't the point of my amends. "But I do want to know: is there anything I can do to make things right between us?"

Jack had been listening intently, and now he spoke. "Well, I have just one thing to say. Maybe two."

My heart sank.

"I love you so much, Heather," he said, smiling. "And I forgive you! Completely."

It was a grace I didn't deserve. And it was a grace that still bears fruit. I've worked long hours with Jack since that conversation, and—with those dark things in the light—I swear, he's more fond of me than before.

It was my first big lesson in the amazing power of making amends.

• eighteen •

A PILLOWCASE OF GRACE

As Halloween approached, several of our neighbors let us know that families from all over town ferried their kids here to trick or treat. Supposedly, parents liked the Victorian-era houses, the enormous trees, sparse traffic, and the old-fashioned, wrought-iron lampposts that line our unusually wide street (built big enough for a horse and carriage to turn around in).

"They come in droves," one neighbor warned.

Dave and I should have asked, *How many is a* drove, *anyway?* But we didn't. We assumed that *droves* meant dozens, possibly. So we overprepared. We bought enough candy for at least sixty children. This would be our first Halloween on Tejon Street, and we were looking forward to it.

The doorbell didn't ring once all evening. That's because from six o'clock on, an endless stream of children made it impossible to leave the porch or shut the front door. We ran out of candy three times, forcing several emergency trips to Safeway.

Droves meant hundreds—more than five hundred, actually.

I had never seen so many trick-or-treaters in my life. I saw the

Energizer Bunny with his drum, I saw the ghost of Raggedy Ann, and I saw untold skeletons. I saw babies in adorable but warm getups—lions and tigers and bears. And thanks to a new friend of Dave's—a single guy who came over with a truly ghoulish troll mask—I saw babies cry.

Here the kids would come in groups of six or ten at a time, then halfway up the walkway to our porch, a youngster among them would catch sight of the terrible troll—and suddenly freeze. Then wobble. Then burst into tears.

And then I'd go running out to try to comfort him and give him candy and apologize to the parents.

When Dave's friend finally took a break from making kiddies cry, my husband took over. He liked the power, I think. The kids approach you differently when you're in costume—there's some chance of respect.

Early in the evening, we were overgenerous with the candy. Once, a pirate came knocking who, along with his friends, looked to be about twelve. On the cusp of too old, but not quite yet. His last year, I was guessing. He held out his pillowcase and told me that he thought he should get extra candy because he was good-looking.

"Really?" I asked, charmed. "So, is that working for you?"

"It sure is!" he said.

I gave him a double portion.

After he bounded off, I thought of my younger son, Nathan, who always liked himself, too. Where do they come from, these confident ones?

Nathan was nine years old when I married Dave, and the boys and I moved over the mountains to the small central Oregon town where Dave lived and worked. A few days before the big move, Nathan came to me in tears. He said he'd changed his mind. He didn't want to move.

I was stunned by his about-face. He and Dave's daughter, Jana, had been begging us to get married for more than a year now. The two were inseparable, both tow-headed and blonde, and they were occasionally mistaken for twins.

"What do you mean you don't want to move?" I asked. "I thought you couldn't wait."

"What about my friends?" Nathan wailed, tears streaming down his pink, freckled cheeks.

"Oh, honey," I told him, pulling his gangly little body in for a hug. "You'll make lots of new friends at your new school! You'll see. I promise."

"No!" he said, pulling away and shaking his head at me. "No, Mom. What will my friends do without *me*?!"

§

At some point during the melee of Halloween evening, Nicole came over. She arrived wearing a sparkling tiara. She still wasn't allowed to be with her kids without Children and Family Services' supervision. So they were trick-or-treating with her estranged husband. Nicole brought along another woman who happened to be living in the same halfway house.

At first, I felt self-conscious about my comfortable home on my pretty street. But I could tell that neither of these women held my good fortune against me. They were grateful, they said, to be somewhere fun on Halloween. The new woman swiped at tears and looked away when she admitted that like Nicole, she, too, had temporarily lost custody of her kids.

I got them both some cider, and we sat on our enclosed front porch in the dark with a candle. I was wearing my striped witch hat, which I'd bought at a thrift store earlier that day.

Eventually, my new editor friend stopped by, too. There was a moment, when I saw us out on the porch reflected in the glass, when I thought to myself: *I am someone with friends. I am someone with people on her porch, and we are all happy to be here.*

I found it amazing how easy it was to feel our common bond as women and to forget that addiction had brought us together.

⑤

While the evening passed and legions of kids came and went, I thought about the last ten years' worth of Halloweens. I couldn't remember more than a few details. I knew that Dave and I had gone to a party or two at neighbors' homes back in Oregon. I knew that I drank. And I knew that I figured I *should* drink plenty, since it was Halloween. But I was never really *there*. Not present. Not really.

Then my mind leaped naturally to the one Halloween I *never* fail to remember—the one when I was seventeen, a senior in high school, and newly pregnant with Noah. Tom and I had decided to have the baby and to get married over Christmas break. And for some stupid reason, we chose Halloween night to break all this news at once to his mother.

With no warning, we sat her down at her kitchen table and crashed her world. I remember that she was crying a great deal, and yet through her tears, she continued to get up when the doorbell rang to hand out candy to happy children. Children who weren't pregnant. Children who weren't breaking their mothers' hearts on Halloween night.

Tom's mother was fairly certain that my pregnancy and our plans to marry would destroy her son's promising life and future. "What about his football scholarship?" she asked in a choked voice. "What about Tom's going to college?"

I didn't see the problem, I told her. Yes, Tom was in line to get a scholarship to play PAC 10 football. But this meant that his college would be free! He could still play. He wasn't pregnant, I was.

Now, I'd like to go back in time and smack myself for being so glib. Every Halloween since, I have wondered if she, too, is reminded of that painful night all those years ago. I wonder if she recalls the three of us sitting there at her kitchen table, and her own tears, and us acting like it was all kind of turning out okay. No big deal.

Ironically, a little over seven months later when I gave birth to Noah, it was Tom's mom who cried tears of joy all the way to the hospital. In fact, her reaction became such a beloved family story that when he was little, Noah would ask to hear it over and over: "Tell me 'bout how Grandma cried when I got born!"

I thought of Noah, now twenty-five years old. I pictured him sitting at his work many states away, half stoned or drunk, selling fitness equipment over the phone. I pictured him playing video games all night and cursing his stupid, pointless life. I wondered, *Does he ever still think, "But Grandma Mary was so happy when I was born that she cried all the way to the hospital..."?*

I remembered a Halloween when Noah wore Tom's UPS shirt to go trick-or-treating. How serious he looked. How somberly he viewed the world, even then. How in his oversized brown shirt with an empty box in his hands for candy, he already looked like he was carrying something too heavy for him.

§

On this Halloween, things gradually began to settle down on our street at about nine. It was a school night, after all.

But I was sad to see it end. I wished mummies and ghosts and bumblebees would knock on my door more often. I would give them candy, I told myself. I would keep a bowl ready at all times.

And why not? Why not let kids dress up at will and go door to door hoping for something good?

The next morning, I woke up to a favorite reading in my daily Bible. It was the one from Hebrews 4:16, about how we can come boldly to the throne of grace for help. It was such a familiar passage, and yet the word *boldly* gave me pause. If the whole idea of grace is that it can't be earned or deserved, why on earth would I come boldly, as if it was expected?

I was also struck by the incongruity of a throne being a place of grace. Thrones are by nature intimidating. Kings mete out judgment from thrones. You could get killed just for having the gall to *approach* a throne uninvited.

Would God really have us stride unabashedly into His presence, marching right up to His gilded seat of power as if we have grace coming to us? Where does one get that kind of audacity?

I was usually more inclined to approach God like my dog, Edmund, approaches me after he's gotten into the garbage again—skulking, ears pinned back with guilt. Since my relapse, this was exactly how I felt, not just about God, but about myself.

Plus, how could I possibly rush God's throne to get grace when I had misspent it so much in the past?

〄

After my coffee and quiet time, I put on a light jacket, and Dave joined me for a quick walk with Edmund. It was sunny but brisk. We took Edmund down the alley, and eventually he found the spot that smelled like the exact right spot. Afterward, he kicked the leaves and dirt behind him, as if to reestablish his dog dignity.

All along our walk, Dave and I noticed the signs of Halloween past. Right in front of our house, we found two Kit Kats and a lollipop a child must have dropped. Someone's green nylon scarf was hanging on the front of our white picket fence. It was hard to say if it belonged to a pirate or a princess.

Dave laughed as he pulled it free. "Earlier this morning I saw glittery angel wings floating down the street in the wind," he said.

I loved that picture. I thought that if I had been Dave, I would have found a way to catch the wings. I would have chased them down the street for several blocks, if need be. I wanted angel wings lying about my house somewhere.

Later, I wondered when the little girl discovered she'd lost her wings. Was she home by then? Did she run outside and look around? And did her parents comfort her by saying, *That's okay, honey, next year we can make you new wings*?

Of course, I was taught that angels don't have wings. And I happen to know that it really bothers some Christians if you don't get that right. Apart from prophetic passages about cherubim or seraphim, the whole wing thing is nowhere in Scripture, they say. Angels can be white and glowing, but they never, *ever*, have wings.

I guess this makes sense, that an angel doesn't need wings to fly. But I also get it, why they got added on. And I get why a little girl might like to be an angel.

ｓ

A few days after Halloween, I opened my Bible again, and my eye caught a line about Jesus being accused of being a drunkard (Luke 7:34, New International Version).

I'd known for years that this was in the Gospels somewhere, but I'd never stopped to consider the implications. I knew Jesus had performed his first miracle at a wedding, turning water to wine, and I knew he hung out with drunks. But I'd never thought about how many people mistook him for one.

The idea amused me. It also made me wonder: Exactly how

much did the Son of God drink? And does this mean Jesus knows what it feels like to be tempted to drink too much?

The question prompted me to go back to that passage about coming boldly to the throne room. And there it was: "For we do not have a high priest who is unable to empathize with our weaknesses, but we have one who has been tempted in every way, just as we are" (Hebrews 4:15, NIV).

Tempted in every way *just as we are*. Really? Empathizing? You mean that Jesus wasn't tempted only in a theoretical way, but in a *real* way? That would mean He knew what it felt like to find Himself gripped by the urge to indulge when He knew He should abstain. Did He ever want to alter or escape reality, too? Did Jesus feel an inner emptiness ever?

I choose to think so, even though we know he never sinned. This passage makes it clear that it was the actual, experienced pain of His temptation that makes Him able to help us: "Because he himself *suffered* when he was tempted, he is able to help those who are being tempted" (Hebrews 2:18, NIV; emphasis added).

Wow. How does that work? And how many years had I never understood what this was saying?

ↄ

It wasn't until I was on the porch taking down decorations that I came across my witch hat. I flashed back to Halloween and all of those kids charging up to our door, expecting something for free. Not because they thought they deserved it. Because they knew we wanted them to come, hoped they would come—expected them to come for candy.

When I was young, my siblings and I wouldn't dream of using a measly bucket for our candy—we used pillowcases. And we'd stuff them. And we'd run, breathless, from house to house. Our family was always poor, candy was a huge luxury, and Halloween was almost as good as Christmas.

Maybe this is a picture of how God wants us to come to Him, too. Anxious to arrive, breathless with a good kind of greed for a grace more generous than we could possibly deserve.

And what if He wants us to rush to Him boldly not because of what it says about our worthiness, but what it says about His? Maybe He sees all of us coming from afar off—trolls and witches and angels with missing wings—and He wants us to come more than we ever could. Because we're beloved. Because He can't imagine what He'd do without us.

nineteen

PENANCE BY POTATOES

Just before Thanksgiving, my mother and my stepdad Jon (yep, the same one) and their enormous horse-sized dog, and their two cats, and all of my mother's stuff moved to the Springs to be near us.

I hadn't lived anywhere close to these people, sort of on purpose, since I moved out when I got married at seventeen.

But when my sister decided to follow me to the Springs, she thought it would be a good idea for my mom and Jon to come, too. She reasoned that if anything happened to my stepdad, if he passed first, my mom would have both her daughters nearby.

I would never have let such a thing happen if I'd still been drinking. But now, I went along with the idea. I was trying to live a more spiritual and generous life, giving other people grace, looking for ways to serve them.

They hadn't even started unpacking when my mom invited me to a thrift store to see a couch she had to have. Not that she needed a couch. But she needed to look at a couch, imagine a couch, and think about buying a couch. She has always been obsessed with garage sales, estate sales, and decorating her house—no, *filling* her house.

When I was still drinking, I was hard on her about it. I'd tell her that all she had to do was put price tags on things and she'd have a store.

Now it occurred to me that she feels a compulsion to get a good deal and collect things because she grew up with so little. She lived in a horrible housing project through most of her childhood and shared a bed with her mother until she was eighteen.

Plus, bargains are what give her that same jolt I used to get from a drink. She'd much rather find a yard of vintage fabric in the Goodwill bin for pocket change than be given a hundred dollars.

For that first trip to the Goodwill, I invited Nicole to join us. She and my mother could both win competitions for shyness. Nicole didn't speak. She trailed us, wearing her usual wardrobe—a hooded sweatshirt with the hood up. Every time I turned around to look at her, she'd smirk. And I would roll my eyes. *Isn't this fun? Look! Old stuff! Used stuff!*

๑

The bigger consequence of my parents moving here was that I would be living near my stepdad. Whereas before I never saw Jon more than once a year or so, now I'd be forced to interact with him on an almost weekly basis.

There was irony in the timing. It meant that now I would be able to make my amends to my mother and stepdad directly, instead of over the phone.

One aspect of Step 9 that I didn't grasp or understand until it was happening to me had to do with the reciprocal nature of forgiveness.

Even though we don't necessarily ask people to forgive us when we make amends, we always hope they will. And something about putting yourself in the posture of acknowledging your wrongdoings and indebtedness to others makes you keenly mindful of your role on the other side of the forgiveness equation.

As I continued to slowly work my way through Step 9, I found myself reluctantly contemplating the question of how thoroughly or deeply I was willing to forgive others. When it came to people who had harmed me in the past, my stepdad was at the top of the list.

Since my mother stayed with Jon after discovering his voyeurism, I had been forced to abide his continued presence in the same house until I moved out at seventeen. In retrospect, I was still young and naïve enough to not grasp what a huge thing it was to ask this of me. It's amazing what you accept when you have no power.

We avoided each other as much as possible.

After Tom and I got married, we moved from Washington State to Eugene, Oregon, so Tom could play football and go to college. It was easier then to keep a comfortable, polite distance. I saw my stepdad on rare occasions and random holidays and never for more than a couple days.

Over the years, Jon noticeably changed. He softened. He went out of his way to help any of us kids with anything we needed. He turned into a fabulous, beloved grandpa. But I still cringed if he so much as touched my back affectionately.

Once, when Tom and I had first moved to Eugene and we were desperately poor and struggling, there came an awful morning. Because Tom's football scholarship prohibited him from working, and I was at home with baby Noah, we were constantly broke. The day came when we literally didn't have gas money for Tom to drive to school, nor did I have money to operate the laundry machine so I could wash some of Noah's diapers.

On that particular morning, I went to our mailbox and found a strange envelope with my stepdad's childish, cramped writing on it. He couldn't spell to save his life. Inside was some cash and a Chevron credit card. And a note filled with misspellings about how he found seven dollars and thought he'd send it to us.

I appreciated the gesture, but I didn't recognize yet that he was trying to pay penance.

ॐ

By the time I was in my early twenties, I was coming unraveled at the seams with regard to sex and men. Despite a perfectly normal sexual appetite before marriage, almost immediately after, I could no longer bear for Tom to touch me sexually. If he even kissed me softly, I wanted to kill him. If I forced myself to have sex with him, it was all I could do not to rake his eyes out.

Eventually, I got into therapy. I learned that I was subconsciously projecting rage at my stepdad, and at men in general, onto my husband. At one point, my therapist told me that I needed to confront not just my stepdad, but my mom, too. Take her to task for her part in the past. For not protecting me.

By now, my sister was dealing with similar issues in her own way. So we came up with a plan wherein she and the two of them would all come to Oregon to visit us.

Shortly after they arrived, my sister and I broke the news that we needed to talk. And not about the weather, grandkids, or Mom's latest garage sale find.

We sat both of them down on the couch and told them they needed to hear us. Speaking one at a time, we each said our piece about the past. Katherine tried to be kind—or at least that is her memory, and it would make sense, since she's sensitive and caring that way.

But my memory is that I held nothing back. I accused my mother of being complicit and allowing my stepdad to do what he did. I accused him of being the pervert that he was.

I brought up the time my sister pulled her car into the carport and almost ran over Jon because he was lying on the ground peering through a basement window into my bedroom. I reminded my mother how when my sister told her what happened, she'd made up some excuse for him.

Naturally, they were both caught off guard. To their credit, they took it. They listened, and they said they were truly so sorry. They agreed with it all, which made it better and worse, too. It's harder to get your rage out at someone when they are weeping and apologizing.

My mom reminded us that Jon went to counseling. His face was bright red, and at one point he broke down crying. You could tell that he was genuinely ashamed and mortified beyond bearing.

At some point, when there was nothing left to say, my sister, my mother, and I walked to the store to get potatoes we needed for dinner.

It was a very long walk. I don't know why we didn't take the car. My mother was still tearful and trembling. At Albertsons, I chose a five-pound bag of potatoes. On the way home, we let my mother carry the bag. She was considerably overweight at the time, and obviously struggling—huffing and puffing.

But what I most vividly recall is my determination *not* to take the bag of potatoes from her. The more I could tell how hard it was for her to manage the load, the more it meant to me that she carry it all the way home.

Worried my sister would intervene, I tried to telepathically relay a message in no uncertain terms to her brain: Don't you *dare* offer to carry the potatoes. *Don't you dare!*

Amazingly, she didn't. We were sisters in synch that afternoon.

My mother carried the potatoes all the way back to my house, where Jon mashed them to serve with dinner. He was a cook by profession, and so he was good at that. He'd whip them so hard and fast that his hands blurred.

Now, whenever I buy a bag of potatoes, I think of the burdens we carry. And the relief of finally setting them down.

§

After that painful exchange, I was convinced that I had forgiven my stepfather. I'd made a conscious decision to be free of the ball of hate that I felt toward him. I agreed to trust vengeance to God, and I released him.

But that didn't mean that I felt comfortable or affectionate toward him. It also didn't mean that I didn't still carry traces of resentment, which is natural. Because it was awkward not to, I usually hugged him good-bye when we left their house, but it was something I had to do quickly and without thinking.

Now, especially since my sister wasn't joining them here for at least six more months, I would not only see them regularly, Dave and I would be the only family in town. It was up to us to make them feel welcome. With Dave, there was never any question. Parents are parents. You respect them. You help them. You go there for dinner when they invite you and you invite them in return.

At least at first, this was more of a stretch for me.

But in doing so, I slowly came to recognize the enormous shame that still lay under the surface of everything my stepdad did for us—his constant determination to drive anywhere, cook anything, or in any way serve us and our kids at the drop of a hat.

Shame was something I understood.

☼

Around this time, Nicole went back to treatment again in Pueblo. It unnerved me that she seemed to treat it so casually—like just another something on her to-do list.

She wanted me to come and see her, so I drove back down to Pueblo and Club Manor Drive. Even though nothing about the place had changed, I couldn't believe how strange it felt to be there again.

I noticed that the living area still smelled like popcorn. Nicole and I sat outside, on the same picnic table I'd sat on before. As usual, Nicole smoked. Her frizzy hair wasn't in a pert ballerina knot atop her head this time—it was wild and, I thought, beautiful.

For some reason, I felt compelled to talk to her about her father again. But this time I totally left God out of it. Forget God. It's about you. It's about how holding on to his horrible crimes keeps them and him *attached* to you. It's about that stinky ball of shame that you lug around with you—because of what *he* did.

Nicole took a drag on her cigarette and eyed me with suspicion. In the shadows behind her blue eyes, I saw her anger still burning bright.

After about ten minutes of futile discussion about her dad, I understood that there was nothing I could say. Facing such horrors, much less forgiving them, wasn't something Nicole could do yet. Forgiving, I think, is a little like giving birth—you'd never willingly let something so painful happen unless your body forced you to. And Nicole just wasn't in hard enough labor yet to heave this mass of bitterness from her soul.

I suspected that delaying such an event was the goal of her drinking and drugging. I shuddered to think what her hatred might look like one day if she insisted on carrying it forever. If she could do so without dying.

෨

Prior to visiting Nicole, I'd been reading *The Glass Castle* by Jeannette Walls. It's a memoir about a girl who grows up so poor and desolate that you can't put the book down without worrying for her in the meantime. The night before, I read how the family got a ham. They ate the ham for days and days. They cut it off in chunks as it sat on the counter (they had no refrigerator). After about a week, the author noticed that the ham had maggots swarming on it.

Just cut off that part, the mother told the daughter. It's fine underneath that.

This story reminded me of my uncle Richard, my stepdad's brother, who jumped out of a plane wearing a parachute that didn't open and broke almost every bone in his body. He was in a body cast for forever and he was itching like wild and finally when they took off the cast, he was infected with maggots.

My mother insists now that it wasn't Richard but another of my stepdad's brothers who got maggots. But the point stands. The maggots found an uncle. And they found that ham. And I think they have found the carcass of Nicole's father that she carries around with her.

Finally, it was time to go. I told Nicole I loved her, knowing she wouldn't return the sentiment. She swore she just couldn't.

Then, against my better judgment, I made a final, halfhearted appeal. "All I know is your dad will pay someday in some way," I told her. "Let God take vengeance. Get out of the way! What if He wants to smite your father like he did Lot's wife when she looked back, but you're still clinging so hard to your father that God can't do what he wants to?"

She laughed. "I'm serious!" I said. "What if your insistence on punishing your dad all by yourself keeps God from punishing him in a more perfect way?"

I hadn't planned this speech, and I wasn't even sure I agreed with my own theology. So I stopped myself from going further. What I wanted to add but didn't was, *What if the fullness of judgment you long to have passed on your father gets passed on you, too? What if the three kids you've neglected—who are tearful and starving for love and not allowed to hug you without your permission—grow up and don't give a rip about what your father did to you?*

I drove home sad. Every exit invited me to stop and take a drink. And every exit I passed by without turning off reminded me that some of us make it, and some of us don't. And life on earth is nothing if not unfair.

ᔥ

Meanwhile, my mother and Jon kept inviting us to dinner and vice versa.

Looking back now, I see how I softened toward my stepdad. Even though he had only an eighth-grade education, he loved to read. Huge, thick books. It was the oddest thing. He always made a point of checking out the *New York Times Book Review* from the library. One Father's Day, I bought him a subscription to the *Review* that would come in the mail.

For the next two years, I wrote Jon cards for his birthday or holidays, where I thanked him for the wonderful meals he made, for being a wonderful grandpa, and being so good to my mom these past two decades. I made a point of telling him the past was forgiven.

One day, I casually mentioned to one of my friends in recovery that Dave and I were planning to go to my mom and stepdad's for dinner on Sunday night for one of my stepdad's famously huge ten-course meals.

Her face instantly flashed confusion. "So this is a *different* stepdad than the one who..." (It's funny how people never want to say it.)

"The one who was a voyeur," I offered. "Yes, it's that one."

"Really?" She couldn't grasp it. "You still speak to him? Your mom is still married to him?!"

I heard myself trying to explain how many years ago that was. How Jon had begged forgiveness and got counseling. How good he had been to my mother in the decades since then. How he adored his grandkids and was the ideal grandpa. I even found myself re-counting how he'd never made it past eighth grade and how when he was little his big brothers put out their cigarettes in his ears.

But I could tell my friend didn't get it. And I was pretty sure that having once asked my mother to do penance for the past by lug-ging a bag of potatoes wasn't going to impress my friend, either.

I understood. When parents make the kind of mistakes that mine did, it's easier to make their villain status permanent than it is to recognize they're screwed-up people in need of forgiveness.

Having kids of your own helps. Becoming a drunk mother in need of her own redemption puts a whole new spin on your per-spective.

Once you've experienced terrible failure as a parent and been handed your own enormous bag of potatoes, you realize that your parents did the best they could with what they'd been given. You quit revisiting the past and invite yourself over for Sunday dinner.

Finally, you sit down at the table with everyone else, where you belong.

ဖ

My parents had been living here around two years when they took a trip back to Washington State. They rarely traveled, but this trip had seemed especially important to them to make. They saw my stepdad's sister and all of his remaining family. They visited the house on Camano Island, which they missed terribly. Jon hugged his favorite trees, ones he'd planted two decades before.

He went to visit his mother's and brother's graves.

They flew back into Denver in the middle of a snowstorm. Someone at a gas station talked them out of driving south to the Springs—too dangerous. So they checked into a hotel near the airport. Then they went next door to a restaurant, where my stepdad ate what he told my mother was the best steak of his life.

In the middle of the night, my mom got up to use the bathroom. She heard a strange thump. Rushing back into the room, she found Jon lying halfway off the bed, dead. She tried to revive him, and the paramedics came, but it was over. He went exactly the way he was always telling everyone that he would: "A quick death and a good-looking corpse."

He was sixty-seven, which seems so young to me now.

He is very much missed.

twenty

WEEKEND FROM HELL

Not long after my parents moved here, and two months after my relapse, Dave and I planned to fly all five of our grown kids here to the Springs for Thanksgiving.

I thought I was ready.

Before the kids came, Dave and I talked about the drinking issue. All of the kids were now of drinking age and they all drank. Only Noah was a problem drinker, though. So should we just say "no drinking" this weekend? Not have it in the house?

My sponsor Kate thought so, and Dave was more than willing. But I wouldn't hear of it. The thought of depriving anyone else of drinking in order to make things easier for me just didn't sit right with me. I couldn't spend the rest of my life avoiding alcohol so that I wouldn't want to drink alcohol. I wanted to learn how to be okay with it around. In recovery we're told that if we are spiritually fit, we can go anywhere, including bars, if we have good reason to be there.

In retrospect, my decision was based on wishful thinking. I wanted to be immune to alcohol. And I was still in the habit of projecting onto other people how *I* would have reacted in years past if I'd gone somewhere for a weekend and there was no alcohol available—because there was a drunk among us. I would have hated that person.

So, when we did all the grocery shopping in advance of the kids' arrival, Dave bought wine and beer. Even though four of the five aren't alcoholic, they were in their twenties. And like most people in their twenties, they liked to drink and hang out and drink some more.

As usual, Noah drank more than anyone. He showed up at our door wearing a scowl that pretty much stayed in place all weekend. He looked terrible, at least forty pounds overweight. Clearly he was miserable, and it broke my heart to see him in such obvious emotional pain.

Noah loved and hated all of us in equal measure. He has always gotten along with his stepsiblings well, and over the years we'd experienced an astonishing absence of the kind of arguments and conflicts blended families and stepsiblings are famous for. Still, in Noah's mind, he was the loser child, the burnt piece of toast in the bunch. He was convinced that all his siblings were far more successful, likeable, well-adjusted, and attractive.

His younger brother, Nathan, had always been an especially hard pill for Noah to swallow. On the one hand, he adored his brother utterly. But he also hated the way life, sports, girls, college, and everything else seemed to come easily for his brother. Nathan didn't have to work at being happy; he woke up that way.

I could tell Noah was trying, that he wanted the weekend to go well. But given the drinking and all the family dynamics, something was probably bound to go wrong.

It came during a game of Speed Scrabble on the second evening. The conflict had to do with whether or not two-letter words were allowed. Noah, having drank too much—having passed through predictable stages from more relaxed and affable to becoming angry and on edge—exploded.

He stood up and began to yell at Nathan and call him this and that, reinforcing his words with his middle finger. He stomped up the stairs, a giant having a tantrum, and left the rest of us stunned, feeling sick and sad. What to do? Who should talk to him? Was this going to ruin the whole weekend?

It needn't have ruined anyone's weekend, but I made sure it ruined mine. I spent the rest of the visit trying and failing to make Noah feel better. I ached for him, noticed every flinch, every grouchy comment or hostile look. He didn't want to be touched or loved. He was consumed with obvious remorse and self-loathing.

The next day we went for a hike, and as usual, Dave herded everyone along, even if some of us didn't want to go. "Some of us" would be Noah and, by virtue of wanting to protect him, me. You could tell he was feeling horrible, hungover, and angry about feeling coerced to go hiking. He walked alone, lagging behind or charging ahead, staring at the ground, resentment emanating from him.

The rest of the kids tried not to notice and act cheerful. It was a sunny, glorious day. But I couldn't enjoy it. Anxious to appease and comfort Noah, I tried to communicate to Dave that we shouldn't hike too long or go too far.

Dave either didn't get it or wouldn't have it. When we came to a fork, I suggested we take the shorter trail, which would keep the hike a reasonable length in my mind. Dave, who has never taken a short hike in his life, disagreed and pressed on.

Rage. Ridiculous but oh so real, white-hot rage consumed me for the rest of the hike. I told myself an old, untrue story about how much Dave caters to his kids over mine. How insensitive and pigheaded he was. How much of a totally selfish jerk he was. Back home, Dave kept trying to make up with me, but at the same time,

I could tell he wasn't inclined to make his whole day about my nasty mood, much less Noah's. He was trying to enjoy his kids. And the fact that he could still do so when I was so angry at him inflamed me.

At some point in the late afternoon, I was in the kitchen and a bottle of red wine was open on the counter and no one was around.

I grabbed the bottle and took a gulp, then stood there, debating. I desperately wanted to empty the bottle. I told myself that if anyone noticed, I could say I had thought they were done with it and had poured it down the sink.

My heart was aching with anger, and every nerve in my body was tense. I told myself, and it just might have been true, that I had never wanted to get drunk, to find oblivion and wipe out my anger with alcohol, so badly in my life. The smell of red wine—the spicy, dark promise of relief wafting from the green lip of that bottle...

Dear God, help me. This time, the idea of sneaking was way more powerful than it had been in Oregon in that hotel room when the minibar was calling my name. Or at the beach when the beers beckoned in the fridge. Unlike the relapse in the Minneapolis airport, I didn't want to drink at Dave and punish him. I was dying to drink—for me—and have no one ever know.

But eventually, they would know. Because I wouldn't be able to lie and stay sober. I can't explain how I knew this, but I did. I think it was finally dawning on me what a powerful role shame and lying and secrets had played in my alcoholism.

I stood there in the kitchen, the taste of my single gulp lingering, tingling my mouth, wonderful and maroon on my tongue.

I prayed, "God help me," even though I wasn't at all sure I wanted Him to. But He must have wanted to, is all I can think. In the next moment, with the next breath, that red wine suddenly smelled like a bloody slit throat gaping open and waiting for me to climb inside. The scent turned as bitter as the lies that were in my mind.

I couldn't go back. I set the bottle down.

Later, I was stunned to realize that even with my recent relapse in Minneapolis, even with Noah dying in front of me, even with everything I had at stake in my sobriety, I could still come so close to drinking.

Today, if I took a single gulp of wine, I would consider that a relapse, not a close call. I would tell my sponsor and it would be a big, huge deal. But at the time, a single sip seemed meaningless, and I chalked it up to a victory.

Ironically, had I taken that gulp more seriously at the time, I have no doubt that my next impulse would have been, *Oh well, then screw it. I might as well drink.* And I'd have been off on another binge.

ॐ

As Thanksgiving weekend came to a close, it was clear to everyone that Noah's mood was so toxic that it was scary. We gave him a wide berth. But inside, I was in agony. My motherly heart felt like it was breaking every single minute, over and over and over.

It didn't help that we'd learned from Noah that he had recently quit his well-paying job selling exercise equipment. He had even admitted to us that for months he got up every morning and smoked dope, then came home and smoked dope during his lunch break from work. Then at night he drank himself into oblivion. And then he got up and did it again the next day.

He had absolutely no idea what he would do now. How he would pay the rent on his apartment. Or buy food. Or what he would do about a job, if anything.

I saw where this was going. I saw my father in my son. And I saw the dark, brooding specter of suicide nipping at Noah's heels. I spent most of the weekend silently hysterical, just going through the motions.

Later, I would learn that the only reason Noah was still alive that Thanksgiving was because the particular apartments he lived in at the time didn't have a garage.

ᔕ

As the kids were preparing to go and everyone was packing, Dave suggested that we try to talk to Noah. He wanted to make sure my son didn't leave without hearing us say clearly that we loved him.

When I asked Noah if he'd come sit on the front porch with us, he glared at me. "You're mad at me."

"I'm not mad at you," I said, sighing deeply to show that I was exasperated.

"I feel like I'm in trouble or something."

"You're not in trouble," I told him. "We just love you and we want to talk to you."

He abruptly rose from where he'd been slumped on the couch and stomped out to the porch. We all sat down, Dave and I turning our chairs to face Noah.

Dave asked him what we could do to help.

"Nothing," he said, putting his face in his hands, shaking his head. "I'm just a total f——up. Obviously. I'm a big, fat f—— and I hate myself."

"What's your plan when you get home, Son?" Dave asked.

"I don't know," he said with a groan. "I have no idea."

"Maybe you should think about moving here to Colorado," Dave suggested. "Think about getting sober like your mom."

I hadn't expected Dave to make that offer. It had come up before, and we'd kicked around the idea of extending such an invitation, but given how things had gone this weekend, I was under the impression that we both knew it was totally pointless to consider such a thing or even ask Noah to.

"I've thought about that," Noah said.

What!? Ever since the failed intervention and treatment stay three years ago, I had assumed that getting sober was off the table. And in a way, I wanted it to be. Because I was pretty sure that Noah couldn't bear to try and fail again. The idea terrified me.

We talked for a few more minutes. Dave said something about how he could stay here at the house for a little while until he got a job and got on his feet.

By now, Noah had softened slightly. "I don't know. I'll think about it. But I might want to do that."

I couldn't believe my ears.

After Dave left to take all the kids to the airport, I sat on the couch in stunned silence. And yet, I knew that I wasn't hopeful as much as I was *scared to hope.* Plus, I wasn't sure I wanted Noah to move here. Not because I wouldn't love having him around, but because I dreaded the conflict, the darkness, the frustration of watching him live his life the way he was living it.

For so long, my son had been dying at a distance. He had been making enough money so that he needed nothing from anyone.

Would I now have to watch him die slowly right in front of my face? With me sober, and no way to escape the pain?

I didn't know if I could do that.

twenty-one

TREADING THIS MIRACLE

By Christmas, it was clear that Noah was determined to take us up on our offer. He wanted to move here and try to get sober, he told us, because he didn't know what else to do. He could see no end to the cycle of daily drinking and smoking pot and wanting to die.

The day before Christmas, Dave flew to Oregon so he could see the other kids in Portland and then help Noah drive a U-Haul back to Colorado with all his stuff.

I learned later that on Christmas night, Noah and Nathan went out drinking and gambling. They got into a horrific fight. The next day, they were sick all day and could hardly move. They declined dinner with Dave. But the following day, Nathan helped his brother empty his apartment into the U-Haul.

Naturally, Dave and Noah hit blizzards and mountain passes on their way to Colorado. It took them three days to get here. They arrived on New Year's Eve, just in time to join me at an all-night party for alcoholics in our town. My sponsor, Kate, was one of the guest speakers.

When Noah seemed to enjoy the evening, I felt it again—the threat of hope.

He made himself at home in the guest room and started going to meetings. He got a sponsor. He had been sober and living with us for almost three weeks when I began to suspect that not only was there reason to hope, it was better and worse than that. It was quite possible that an actual miracle was afoot.

One cold, wintry morning, Noah had been up long enough to eat a mixing bowl full of cereal. He was supposed to look for work that day. I was up in my office, journaling on my computer when, from somewhere in the house, I heard Noah singing. A few minutes later, he whistled. I heard him *whistle*!

For so long I had thought that *real* miracles—the big ones, the ones that mattered—involved spectacular things like lame people walking or blind people seeing. As a child, I couldn't understand why God didn't just do some huge dramatic miracle so everyone would know they're supposed to believe in Him.

I used to pester my mother, "Why *not*? Why doesn't He?"

Now I was witness to a miracle that was the sound of my grown, angry, alcoholic son whistling. It was watching this same son hand over all his video games to his brother for safekeeping while he tried to get his life back. It was this same son being willing to do something so mundane and ordinary as walk the dog with his mother in the snow.

That was what happened after I heard him whistle. I went downstairs and asked him if he wanted to come walk Edmund with me, expecting a no but getting a yes. Lately, I couldn't get used to the way he kept saying yes. *Yes, I'll come with you*; *Yes, I'd like to go to a meeting*; *Yes, I'll be there for dinner*—it was as if *Yes* had permanently taken the space where before *No* had always parked.

And so, we got our coats on, and Noah found his huge shoes.

Edmund spotted the signs of a walk and started pogoing high in the air, begging to be leashed. *Tie me up!* he always pleaded. *Oh, please. Tie me up!*

Outside, the brilliance of sun on snow blinded us. Noah and I held up our hands to our foreheads to shield our eyes. "It's so bright!" we declared.

The snow was soft but crystal-like. It was the kind that you could sled in. The kind, I reminded Noah, that used to give Dave dangerous ideas. Back in Oregon, when the kids were still young, he'd tie a toboggan to the back of his car and drive them through mostly empty backstreets, the sled fishtailing behind.

I could never bear to watch. Once, he slammed them into a garbage can accidentally on purpose, and they laughed. They thought it was funny. Their eyelashes would always freeze.

A few moments later, Noah asked me to make Edmund go potty. He always liked to hear me order Edmund to do this because it amazed him when Edmund usually obeyed.

"He already went this morning," I told Noah. And I could see my breath in the air.

⑤

Later that day, I was writing again, and I was trying to find a way to say the miracle that just might be happening with Noah. I was also thinking about Peter, who I'd been reading about that morning. You know the story: how Peter left the boat, believing he could walk on water to Jesus. And for a few steps, he did.

Then comes the part of the story where I always thought, *Don't look down, Peter! Don't look down now!*

But he always did. And he always started to sink, and I always wished that the story would end differently. I couldn't understand how Peter had the faith to set out and then, right in the middle of the miracle—right when he was *living* it—he panicked and sank.

Maybe the middle is always the riskiest part of any miracle, when you're so excited that it's happening that you're afraid to hope it will last. You leave the present to worry about the future and…it all collapses around you.

It occurred to me to wonder if this was the only halfway miracle in the Gospels.

My thoughts about Peter and miracles were interrupted by the sound of Noah starting to play his guitar. Music had always been one of Noah's passions, but he'd quit playing his instruments years ago, when tidal waves of depression came so hard and fast that he could hardly get any good gulps of air in between them.

Now, he must have gone out to the garage and found the guitar case in the pile of various odds and ends where we had stacked his stuff. I couldn't believe it. This was even bigger than whistling. He'd taken the time and the initiative to go out there, open the case, and take out the instrument. From my den, I heard him strumming.

I listened for a minute, pained by hope so strong that it felt like it would choke me. I wanted to freeze the moment forever.

Eventually, I went back to my writing. And Noah kept on strumming. And after a while, it was like a sweet song we were playing together. My music was the tap of my keys, singing *Noah lives, Noah lives,* like he was Jesus back from the dead. I didn't know what Noah's song was about, but I think it was the one we all play when we're simply doing what we love and letting it lead us who knows where.

ରୁ

During these strange winter days, while I dared hope and dared *not* hope for Noah in equal measure, I kept recalling a tragic event that took place when we were still living in Oregon. It happened to friends of our best friends, people we didn't know personally. But it scared me in the way that tragedies passing a little too close to us tend to.

The family in question was active in the Christian community. The mother, like most mothers, prayed often for her children's safety. She had two boys who loved to ski, one thirteen and the other seventeen. One weekend, the two brothers were driving home from a day of skiing. It was warm in the car and they were tired, and the son who was driving fell asleep. Both boys were killed in the ensuing accident.

The story is obviously heartbreaking. And not surprisingly, at the time it challenged my belief in God's commitment to respond to our prayers. A critical part of my faith had always hinged on the idea that my prayers could influence God to intervene in the world. If I just prayed hard enough and often enough, and made sure to throw in plenty of thanksgivings before I made petitions, God would do what I asked.

When God didn't, it meant one of two things to me. The answer was no, for good and loving reasons I might understand later. Or, more likely, I just hadn't prayed hard enough and with enough faith and fervor to move God to act on my behalf. I told myself that it was those little doubts that seeped through the cracks that inevitably spoiled the power and effectiveness of my prayers.

In the past ten years, as the threat of something bad happening to Noah and the likelihood of Noah doing something bad to himself became increasingly, painfully real, I had been beside myself many nights with worry.

I prayed fiercely, often with tears, and in a pleading manner. And then, in case pleading showed doubt instead of the persistence I meant it to convey, I'd backed it up with affirmative statements predicting God's help, as if declaring that my faith was firm made it less like the Jell-O I knew it was.

One would think now that Noah was living nearby and trying to stay sober, I would relax a little. Surely, I should see this recent shift in circumstances—Noah's moving here to get sober—as a clear sign that God had indeed heard my prayers, was moved by them, and was even now in the process of granting some of my most heartfelt petitions.

And yet, I couldn't seem to feel at peace around that idea. I was suspicious of a prayer formula that appeared to have "worked" this time but had so often disappointed me in the past. If the lemons line up on the slot machine once in a hundred times, that doesn't mean the prayer finally worked, does it?

§

One day in January, Nicole asked me to meet her at a coffee shop downtown. She'd been out of treatment for a few weeks now, and she showed up looking wretched. She was shaky, sucking hard on her cigarette like it contained the answer to life.

She told me she knew that I thought she'd been using. But she hadn't. And she resented it that I didn't believe her.

It was near dusk and starting to get very cold. Most people were at home starting dinner by now, but Nicole wanted to linger. Dave called on my cell phone to see where I was. I told him I was with Nicole. I'd be home soon.

But I couldn't figure out why we were even here. She was right about what I suspected. But why accuse me of falsely judging her, when I hadn't said a word?

"Look me in the eyes," I finally told her.

She reluctantly turned her big blues on me and sighed heavily.

"Now, while you're looking in my eyes, tell me that you haven't been using or drinking lately."

She opened her mouth and then shut it again and swore. "Why did you make me look you in the eyes?"

"I had a feeling."

She admitted she'd been doing meth. Because it was a drug that she thought she could get away with. She was pretty sure that when she had a hot UA (urine analysis, required by the Department of Human Services), she could blame it on her cough medicine.

"I didn't want to lie to you," she said. "But if I tell you the truth, then I know I'll end up telling *everyone*."

"Well, I'm not going to tell anyone," I told her. "That's totally up to you. But I gotta tell you, Nicole. I don't get it. What do you even *want*?"

"What do you mean, what do I want?" she said with a smirk. "That's exactly what my therapist asks me."

"That's because it's a good question," I told her. "So, what do you want? What do you want to happen? What do you want for your life?"

She said she wanted to stay clean and sober. She just couldn't seem to.

We talked for another half hour. She spent the entire time picking at the label on her yellow Bic lighter. The coffeehouse staffer came out and told us Nicole couldn't smoke. Even though our table was outside, it was still part of the restaurant. Nicole stood and moved a foot away from the table and kept smoking.

The reason she couldn't get the label off of the lighter was because she had continued to bite her nails down to tiny nubs, like a grade-schooler.

Eventually, she handed me the lighter. "Get that off," she said, as if it was important.

So, I picked it up and scraped at the gummy label until it was gone except for some glue residue. I handed it back to her. "Well, at least the lighter is clean now," I said.

"You're mad at me," she insisted. She sounded exactly like Noah.

"I'm not mad. I worry," I told her.

Exasperated and sad, I walked her to her car. I didn't try to hug her for once, and she didn't hug me. But I did tell her I loved her. I told her sincerely. I told her in a way that I hoped might make it past whatever barriers she had erected in order to not believe in love.

"I love you, too," she said, half-laughing. She knew that I knew that this was hard for her to say.

Many weeks passed before I realized that Nicole and I had really been saying good-bye that day.

After that, she fell out of my life. And I let her go.

🌀

In the meantime, something about watching Noah try, watching him struggle with the raw feelings of new sobriety, broke my heart. At times I felt as if the hope in my bones was too brittle to bear much pressure. A seeming yes from God felt like a double-edged gift that promised great disappointment later.

One day, he called me on my cell phone while I was standing in a used bookstore. I stared at the worn spines of dozens of self-help paperbacks while he admitted to me that he wasn't doing well. He was anxious and depressed. He said he called in sick to work that morning (he'd gotten a job at an insurance company), and now he wished he hadn't, because being home alone all day didn't help.

I don't remember what I said, except that every word sounded hollow and falsely optimistic. After we hung up, I stared at the shelves of books in front of me and marveled that there seemed to be nothing here to help Noah. Nothing to explain to a lost young man struggling to stay sober why life was worth it. I couldn't help wondering how long he could hang on.

I thought of Nicole and my heart dipped further. And I thought of Miguel, too. I hadn't seen him in a meeting for quite a while. Was he still praying in the outhouse, looking in the tiny mirror on the door? In that moment, I just couldn't bear thinking of all the Noahs and Miguels and Nicoles in the world—but I couldn't stop myself, either. *Why* does life have to be so hard? Why do we have to hurt?

On the phone, I wanted to tell Noah not to worry, that help was coming—as if an ambulance was on its way right now. I wanted to tell him, *Hold on! Hold on!*

But hold on to what? I couldn't be certain that anything like help would show up anytime soon.

Later, sitting in my chair at home, it was clear to me that I couldn't carry this ache. I couldn't carry Noah. I couldn't bear the responsibility of praying hard enough to save him, nor could I stand the idea of not trying, nor could I escape my anger at the idea that I just needed to twist God's arm harder to make Him care more.

I began to cry. I let the horribleness of my terror for Noah wash over me. I sobbed over the precariousness of hope. I wailed about the uncertainty—I was tired of feeling like I was about to watch my child fall from a high ledge while knowing that no matter what happened, I wouldn't be able to catch him.

Swiping at tears, I gave in to the familiar urge to pray yet again. Almost angrily, I prayed for God to help Noah stay sober. I thanked God for His part in what good was happening so far—in case He'd had a part. I prayed the rote prayers I had prayed dozens of times, only now I didn't pretend to be convinced; I didn't huff and puff with put-on, playacted fervor and faith. I just asked.

It was what it was.

And then things took an unexpected turn. I felt myself being led where no mother wants to go, deep into the worst-case scenario. In my imagination I was suddenly experiencing what I feared most—losing Noah.

I wept, rocking myself. I had not sobbed this way since that day by my bed in March. It lasted for at least twenty minutes, and in that time I finally arrived somewhere outside of and beyond all my previous attempts to trust God or to pray in faith or to believe the best.

How could I not have understood before that this was my only option? I could not trust God to keep Noah safe or alive or sober. Life had proved to me that God was not to be trusted in this sense. And for the first time ever, I wondered if He expected to be trusted for positive outcomes. If He even demanded to be.

What if God could only be trusted in a way that went far beyond simply trusting Him for any specific result? What if He could only be trusted *with* the outcomes, or despite the outcomes? What if He could only be trusted from the incomprehensible perspective of all eternity?

In which case, I knew what God was asking of me. God was asking me to hand Noah over. Give him up. Let go of him. Let him fall off the ledge. Not just for today, so God could keep him safe. Not just so that I could prove my faith or so that I could feel free from worry or doubt. But hand him over because I choose to trust God *no matter what*.

No matter what is a dagger to a mother's heart. It means your only hope is to surrender all hope. *No matter what* is the place we don't ever want to be forced to reach. And yet in some mysterious way I had. Either I trusted God with Noah's entire life and death in a way that surpassed my limited understanding of what good would look like, or I didn't trust Him at all.

193

As I came to the end of my hiccupping tears, I wondered if I was willing to continue with what had happened here. To adopt a new posture in my prayers of total trust that wasn't attached to outcomes. Was I willing to give up imagining that I could trust God only if my own strength of will and clenched-fist prayers were a successful part of some spiritual bargain?

I didn't resolve all my questions about prayer that day. But something got resolved. It was another small movement from a faith based on my cognitive beliefs to an experiential trust in God that is big enough to make you willing to leave the boat on the impossible hope that in the context of eternity, the present moment makes some kind of beautiful sense, no matter what.

In time, I would gradually give up a great deal of my old way of praying, the kind that took place solely in my head and relied on my intellect. The kind of prayer that piled up words and lists and techniques and rested on the assumption that I could decipher God's will for people—or better yet, determine it by my suggestions.

In its place, I tended more and more to something I don't have a name for except perhaps prayers of surrender. These prayers were focused on openness and acceptance of what is. On letting go of whatever I was clinging to or resisting. Often, though I prayed with great intention in my heart, my prayers didn't involve words.

๑

My worst fears for Noah didn't come to pass. The next time I saw him he seemed better. After six weeks, he moved out of our home and into a tiny apartment in a historic house a mile away. Now I wouldn't see him every day. I couldn't know what he was doing. Or how he was doing. Or if he was still sober.

This was genius.

In the meantime, I came across what I now realized could be called the second half of Peter's boat story. It's at the end of John's Gospel, in the final scene. By now, Jesus has been crucified and his grave found empty. Peter has gone back to fishing, filled with guilt and remorse over his triple-whammy betrayal of Jesus. Peter and some other disciples are out in a boat (probably the same boat), having no luck, when a stranger onshore yells at them to cast their nets on the other side of the boat.

When they do, the nets are so full of fish that they're bursting at the seams.

The huge catch alerts Peter to the man's real identity. "It's the Lord!" he cries. This time, when Peter leaves the boat, he doesn't care a fig about walking on water. He doesn't care about the huge catch of fish. He immediately strips off his clothes, dives into the sea, and then swims with all his heart toward Jesus.

Once back onshore, Peter shares breakfast with Jesus. Amid the aroma of frying fish, another kind of miracle begins to break. This time, the story *does* end differently, and the miracle is complete. Jesus gives Peter the opportunity to affirm his love for Him three times over—once for every time Peter had so shamefully denied him. Gently, lovingly, Jesus restores Peter's calling by asking him repeatedly to "feed my sheep."

In the end, though it was less flashy, wasn't this the only miracle that mattered? And wasn't his swimming toward the Lord he'd so recently, thoroughly, publicly rejected a greater expression of faith and actual trust in the love of Jesus than trying to walk on water could ever be?

I wondered if the same thing could be true for Noah and me. Maybe what mattered most was not wrestling from God a guarantee that my son would experience unbroken, unsinkable sobriety any more than I had. Maybe the real miracle was the confidence of grace—to know that even if we *do* look down, even if we start to drown, God will reach out His hand for us.

Hold on! Hold on!

These days, that's all I can do. I try to stay in the moment. I surrender whatever I cannot control, especially Noah. In the mornings, I wake to the feeling of wet water on the soles of my feet, the sea foam between my toes. The sun is glinting off of the frothy waves, like morning light on new snow. And one day at a time, one step at a time, I'm treading this miracle.

HERE IS WHERE WE GO FROM HERE

S o Mom, how do you explain this thing to people?"

Noah put this question to me the other day while standing in my kitchen eating leftovers from my fridge. He'd recently had poker night with some friends, only some of whom are in recovery. The rest of them drink a lot of beer while they play. Noah says he's happy to show up with his half case of lime-flavored sparkling water.

While I unloaded the dishwasher and Noah munched, he explained that during a recent poker game, one of the guys kept trying to congratulate him for being sober for so long. He said he couldn't imagine having Noah's kind of willpower or strength of character.

"They think I'm sitting there, like, white-knuckling it, Mom!" he told me, laughing. "They think I just resist temptation over and over because I'm a good person or because I have all this willpower. Can you imagine? How do you explain to people that it's not anything like that?"

I nodded in understanding. "It's funny, isn't it?"

So much about how recovery works feels counterintuitive. How *do* you explain to people it has little to do with willpower or being strong, but almost everything to do with knowing that you are weak and powerless? That only when you give up fighting to control your addiction do you give God room to fight *for* you? That when you surrender control, you regain your freedom to choose?

"The other thing people don't get is meetings," Noah told me. "They don't get why you have to keep going and going."

I knew exactly what he was talking about. Sometimes a friend or relative will say: "You're *still* going to those things? Haven't you been to enough of them by now?"

How do you explain that you no longer have to go—you *get* to go? And that it's not because you're slow to catch on that you want to keep going, but because asking another drunk for help, and helping another drunk in turn, helps you stay sober.

Noah, with his six-foot-six inches' worth of appetite, was still working his way through my fridge with clear resolve and obvious pleasure. Now he was on to a drumstick. As I watched him eat, I kept flashing back to how he looked as a gangly toddler when he ate a leg of chicken.

Actually, I thought, *he looked almost exactly the same!*

Noah hasn't had a drink or a drug since the day Dave helped load his stuff in the U-Haul and drove him down here to the Springs. At this writing, that was almost five years ago.

But now, instead of looking bloated, heavy, and sad, Noah looks lean and serious. He still struggles with the ups and downs of life. (Getting sober didn't change his personality overnight any more than it did mine.) Yet these days, Noah not only has a sponsor, he has a couple sponsees of his own—guys he meets with on a regular basis and tries to guide through the steps, just as he was guided by his own sponsor.

Sometimes he comes by the house to ask advice. "What if the

guy doesn't believe in God?" Or, "Do you always do the sixth and seventh step right after the fifth? Or do you wait awhile?"

Such precious concerns! The boy who couldn't get past his own pain and his own worries is now worried about other people's healing journey.

Will wonders never cease? Will miracles never stop rolling in like waves on the beach?

⑤

At a recent meeting, I met a woman who wore a chunky cross necklace and clasped and unclasped her hands nervously in her lap. Clearly a newbie, her voice trembled as she gave a little speech I've heard before.

"I'm a Christian, actually," she said. "I don't know how I ended up with this problem. I know God. But for some reason that hasn't kept me from getting addicted to food and alcohol. I can't believe I'm here."

My heart went out to her. And I wondered for the umpteenth time if we Christians don't make the most miserable addicts. Since we tend to think of addiction strictly as a moral failing, most of us try to pull ourselves up by our spiritual bootstraps. We pray harder, repent more fervently, and fight temptation until we're blue in the face.

When our best efforts prove futile, we feel ever more guilty and ashamed. And confused. Don't we love God enough to quit? Doesn't God love us enough to deliver us?

Meanwhile, to even admit that we have become addicted feels like a betrayal of Christ's work on the cross.

Too often, in order to shield those we love, and to protect God's reputation (and ours), we try to hide our problem. Ironically, our desire to maintain a good witness can turn us into sneaks, liars, and hypocrites. Which then turns us into prisoners of our own egos.

Maybe this is how respected spiritual leaders end up with a CNN tagline that begins, *Disgraced pastor...* Certainly this is also how once joyful Christians can become jaded, miserable ones.

Which brings us to the question I'm asked most often by other Christians: "Why wasn't your faith alone enough to save you from alcohol?"

Had I quit drinking as soon as I realized that I was overindulging, perhaps it might have been. I've heard stories of people who put the bottle down and refused to drink again because they feared what might happen. They have my whole-hearted respect.

But in my case, I plunged ahead until I was caught in a full-blown addiction. These days, instead of viewing addiction as either sin or sickness, I believe it involves both.

We are all sinners, of course. When we battle compulsions and obsessions, we make choices that are fair to call sin. That is, we make choices that offend God and hurt others and ourselves.

But when these behaviors progress to the point of addiction, things get more complicated. Now we're dealing with a condition that includes very real physical, psychological, and spiritual components.

How else but "sick in body, mind, and spirit" could you describe a mother who drinks so much she can't recall anything her husband told her the night before? Who, if she hasn't had enough alcohol, can't get her contacts in her eyes because her hands shake too much? Who, though she imagines she would die for her children, can't quit drinking for them?

During the years of my private hell, I wish someone had sat me down and given me the good news: "You're *not* a uniquely horrible person, Heather. You're mentally, spiritually, and physically sick. And while there is no cure, there *is* a solution."

Instead, I was caught in an endless cycle of trying and failing to conquer my sin. I didn't understand that a sinful compulsion can also be a disease of the body, mind, and spirit. That a spiritual solution that didn't address all these components could treat only one aspect of my malady.

For me, the idea that my alcoholism is a disease is not a means of escaping responsibility, but an invitation to fully embrace a program of recovery specifically designed to treat it.

These days, I see myself as an ordinary person with a physical and mental predisposition that will never go away but that no longer defines my life. And I also know I'm a sinner saved by grace—not just once so I can get into heaven, but every day so I can live sober, happy, and free.

In the past, if you were to ask me, "What went so terribly wrong in your walk with God that you ended up a miserable Christian drunk?" I might have come up with a long and very convincing list.

But today, an equally true answer would be, "Nothing."

Nothing went so wrong that I escaped God's will or His love for me. Nothing went so wrong that it couldn't be a part of my spiritual journey. Nothing went so wrong that God couldn't turn it into something beautiful.

ᔕ

While I was writing this book and it was taking forever and I was frequently tempted to stab my computer screen, God did a kind thing. He kept sending me my reader.

One by one, He plunked women in my path, all of whom had several things in common: they came from some sort of Christian background, they were addicts of some kind, they were mystified as to why their faith hadn't been able to save them, and they wondered how to merge their Christian beliefs with the spiritual tenets of recovery.

We spent hours on the phone, in coffee shops, or sitting on my front porch in rocking chairs discussing recovery and Christianity. How did being an addict shed light on God's will for us? How did what we were learning in recovery contradict what we previously thought was true, or even desperately hoped wasn't true, about God?

We wrestled with difficult topics like surrender, temptation, and the role of grace.

We had spiritual awakenings.

We had breakdowns, too.

We learned that our addictions—crushing and humbling though they may be—remind us of our ravenous appetite for spiritual sustenance. They remind us that we are desperate for nothing so much as we are desperate for God. They remind us that when we think we want a drink or a drug or an emotional fix, when the wind blows through our empty spaces, what we really crave is grace.

For most of us, there was no going back to the safe ground where some of us had stayed for so long, secure in what we believed, satisfied with being "right," and asleep to the promise of spiritual redirection. We were wide awake now, thanks to the pain of addiction. We rightly sensed that the road ahead would be strange and long—that the task of seeking to rediscover God might last not a season but a lifetime.

Some days, we felt like we were going in circles. But a circle goes nowhere only if you stay on its surface. Our plan was to go deeper with each curve and turn, corkscrewing our way into the heart of God.

৯

Annie Dillard once wrote, "I don't know beans about God."

That's how I feel now, too. Like I used to know mountains about God and now I have only a molehill to point to. It seems the larger God becomes in my life, the less I know for sure.

In the years since I got sober, I have wrestled with many of my long-held intellectual assumptions and certainties about God, especially those which now seem contradictory to my actual *experience* of God.

But maybe I don't need to know beans about God in order to have a vital, loving relationship with Him. I can still know His presence and power in my life. I can still rely on Him to keep me sober day by day. I can forgo intellectual certainty and rely on what grace tells me is true of God. I can forgo cleverness and decisiveness in favor of bewildered trust—not because I get it all, but because I know that I can't.

It wasn't until I'd been in recovery for several years that I could look back and see how these questions and doubts compelled me to take the spiritual journey I've chronicled here. It wasn't a direct path—a clean route to God—that I took. I stumbled a lot. I fell on my face. Hard. And even now, my daily journey of faith is messy and unpredictable. Lingering questions still tag along.

But these days, I don't shoo them away. I welcome them, hold their hands, and keep an eye out for answers I may or may not find. Lately, I've come to realize it's the pestering doubts and unresolved issues, not the answers or sureties, that most often lead me forward on the path of grace. So it's fine with me that the final destination, where all the answers are known and understood, is nowhere visible yet.

৯

When I first started meeting with Kate and working the steps, I was baffled by something she'd regularly tell me: "Thank you for helping me stay sober."

Now I understand what she meant. These days, I get to sponsor women, too. And I am often overcome with gratitude for them. Their stories remind me what it used to be like when I was still drinking. Their questions remind me that I don't have all the answers. Their tears remind me that I largely owe my recovery not to a philosophy or a program, but to people I love and who love me in return.

Last week I had breakfast at my favorite bakery with a sponsee named Amy, who was fresh out of treatment. As I nibbled on a peach scone and she on a saucer-sized cookie, I marveled at the change I could already see in her. I noticed how her blue eyes sparkled with clarity and her cheeks were flushed pink with joy instead of alcohol.

She talked excitedly about the new friends she'd made and how much she'd learned about herself and her disease. Then, she sighed, sat back, and admitted that she was scared to be at home. She hated her life and she didn't think she would make it sober.

"But you're doing great, Amy!" I told her. "You're going to be just fine."

"You don't get it," she said. "I don't have a life to come back to. I have zero friends in town, apart from you. I don't have any hobbies. I don't have anything I like to do but drink. Since I work from home all day, I hardly ever leave my apartment. Which used to be such a good thing. But now..."

Aha. I understood. "You turned your house into your favorite bar and now you're forced to live there."

She nodded. "Exactly! Everywhere I turn, I see myself drinking."

I reminded Amy that it takes some time to rebuild our lives so that they reflect and support our new healthy intentions in recovery. I encouraged her to explore new pastimes and to find practical ways to redeem various spaces in her apartment.

But I saw something else behind Amy's eyes, too. The fear that she could not trust herself to be alone with herself.

A consistent hallmark of addiction is that it divides us at our very core. In that awful moment when we truly desire and determine *not* to drink, and then still do, *we have begun to drink against our own will.* The one of us has split into two, and it seems like the better of us has disappeared into the night.

I told Amy how this was my experience of early sobriety. I felt exiled from my better self. I couldn't figure out how to feel like one person again. How do you take a divided soul and make it whole again?

I'm no expert, but I think we do it with God, one day at a time, and gently. We coax home the part of ourselves that was captive to alcohol and in love with her abductor, and we do that by forgiving her. We invite her to face her demons while we hold her hand. We do this until she sees that in order to heal the life she's been fleeing, she must turn and embrace it.

It takes courage not to pick up a drink. But one of the bravest acts of recovery is to stay in the here and now of our most mundane days and try to find God there. To look reality in the eye and open our arms wide to it when what we want to do is run. We redeem the lost ground of our scorched past by living today head-on. We make love. We ride our bikes. We eat old-fashioned soft-serve ice cream.

It seems ironic to me now that the proof of life I was looking for in early sobriety was hiding in these ordinary encounters with reality. I found it in the way my fingertips felt on the silky skin of my husband's back. I found it in the soreness of my sit bones after riding my bike with him. I found it in the bright sound of my son's voice on my answering machine.

I found it right here.

GRATITUDES

This book proved so hard to write that I would have succumbed to despair—begged to be dragged from my desk and locked up somewhere—had it not been for the faith and support of family and friends. For each of them, I will be eternally grateful, especially:

To my husband, David Kopp, who encouraged me from the start. Thank you for being brave enough to let me tell my story (which somewhere along the way became our story) in all its messy glory. Your unflinching belief in me always felt like love. Thank you for telling me a thousand times, "It's going to be all right."

To my son, Noah, who graciously gave me permission to share the parts of his story that overlapped mine. I am forever grateful for your support, love, and friendship. I admire your convictions, your courage, your honesty, and your great taste in TV shows. I could not be more proud of you.

To my son, Nathan, whose support I can't imagine living without. You called regularly to see how the book was going and to cheer me on. You helped me start my blog. You blessed me with a wonderful daughter-in-love. And you have forgiven me so much. I'm so glad I had you!

To Neil, Taylor, and Jana—my children by marriage to Dave. No stepmom could feel more accepted, loved, and supported than I have by you. Really, it's ridiculous how wonderful you all are. That you love me even half as much as I love you is a miracle I may never get over.

To my sister, Katherine Lloyd, my first reader and biggest fan. How could I have done this without you? I couldn't have. Your wisdom, support, prayers, and love have meant the world to me. This book bears witness that my story is better because of you.

To my mother, Gloria Lynch, who always encouraged me to write the truth about our family even when it wasn't pretty. Thank you for being such a huge part of God's redemptive work. Today you are the mother I always wanted, as well as the one I needed nearby while I wrote this book. I love it when you come by for tea.

To my dear brothers, Jim and Andrew—you don't show up much in this book, but I know both of you would show up for me in a heartbeat if I needed you. A special thanks to you, Andrew and Sandi, for loving my blog and being so encouraging.

To my boys' dad, Tom, and his lovely wife, Rachel—thank you for supporting this book, and for bringing so much goodness, grace, and blessing into our family.

To my Westside Women and Serenity Sisters, the keepers of my sanity and sobriety—you save me every day.

To my dearest friends who keep me sane and sober, and feed my soul from the overflow of theirs—sincerest thanks: Carol, for being my spiritual soul mate and greatest encourager; Carrie, for being one of the most authentic, passionate people I know; Cindy, for listening to me, and for being a beautiful example of the promises at work; Connie, for being a mentor, a friend, and a beacon to so many; Gita, for helping me to see and reach for a bigger God; Jamie, for opening up and letting me be part of your journey; Karina, for reminding me what true beauty looks like, inside and out;

Kellie, for being so brilliant, talented, and just plain cool; Kristi, for reaching out and letting me in; Michelle, for being a constant source of light, laughter, and dead-on truth telling; Sandra, for oozing spiritual enlightenment of the most serene kind; Shawna, for showing us all how to cope in tough times with calm and grace; and Skyler, for being a spiritual sister who makes loving God seem both doable and groovy.

To author Susan Isaacs, dear friend and one of the most talented people on the planet. When I needed a sign of hope on the other side of sober, you were a star to guide me. Thank you over and over—and Larry, too. You two are a treasure to both of us.

To Kim Hayes, whose time-tested friendship I treasure. Thank you for loving me through it all.

To Rebecca Sokol, friend of my heart. Your belief in my writing and in this book have meant more to me than you can possibly imagine.

To dear friend and renowned editor Liz Heaney, who read and commented on my manuscript *twice*—I can't thank you enough.

To my first writing buddies, Linda Clare, Melody Carlson, and Kris Ingram. You have cheered me on almost as long as I've been writing. Thank you.

To my book group, which is so much *more* than a book group—Elisa Stanford, Erin Healy, Laura Barker, Susan Miller, Elizabeth Hendricks, Tara Owens, and Rachelle Gardner. I am so grateful for the friendship, encouragement, and wisdom you have shared with me over these past five years.

To our church family at First Congregational, Colorado Springs, for restoring our hope, and making us glad to call this community home.

To everyone at Hachette/Jericho Books who was instrumental in bringing *Sober Mercies* to print, including my fabulous editor,

Jana Burson; publisher, Wendy Grisham; director of publicity, Shanon Stowe; and associate publisher, marketing, Harry Helm.

A special thank-you to my wonderful blog readers at SoberBoots, many of whom have become close friends.

Huge thanks to my amazing agent, Rachelle Gardner. I am so fortunate to have you as both agent and friend. Without your editorial genius and persistence, this book would have been only half realized. I'm deeply grateful.

And finally, I thank God for his presence and daily, extravagant mercies, and for these friends and others he has graciously brought into my life.